D0549507

BEN NEVIS &
GLEN COE

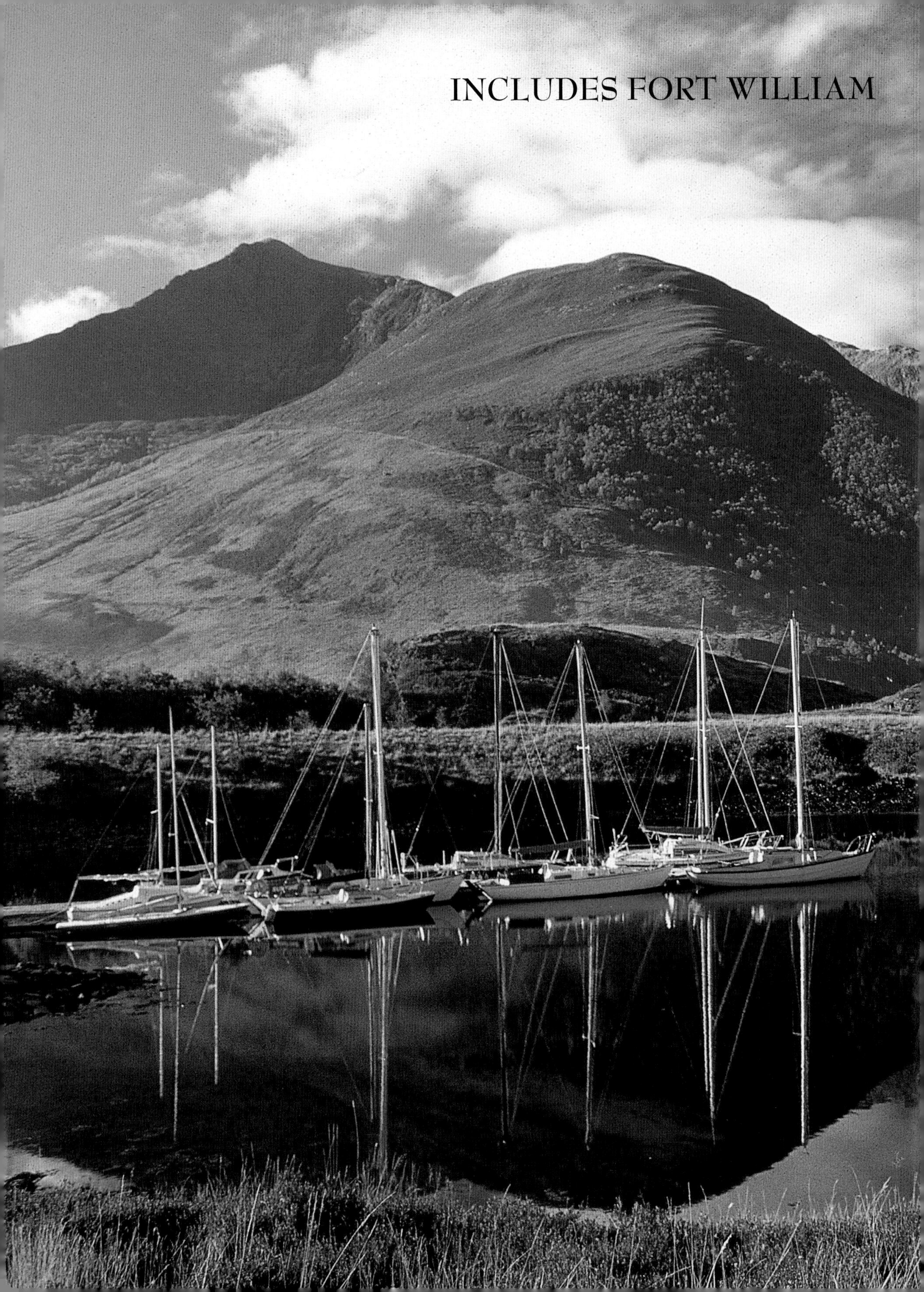
INCLUDES FORT WILLIAM

BEN NEVIS & GLEN COE

ALAN HALL

PEVENSEY GUIDES

TO A' CHAILLEACH

Page 1: The Three Sisters – 'faith,
hope and charity'
Pages 2–3: Beinn Bhàn, 'white peak',
and the Ballachulish Horseshoe, a
mirror image in Loch Leven
Right: Sunset at Rhuda na Glas-lice
Far right: Ben Nevis over Meall
an t-Suidhe from Cow Hilla

The Pevensey Press is an imprint of David
& Charles

Copyright: Text © Alan Hall 2000
Photographs © Alan Hall 2000

First published 2000
Reprinted 2006

Map on page 6 by Ethan Danielson

Alan Hall has asserted his right to be
identified as author of this work in
accordance with the Copyright, Designs
and Patents Act 1988.

All rights reserved. No part of this
publication may be reproduced, stored in a
retrieval system, or transmitted, in any
form or by any means,
electronic or mechanical, by
photocopying, recording or otherwise,
without prior permission in writing from
the publisher.

A catalogue record for this book is
available from the British Library.

ISBN 1-898630-08-9

Page layout by
Martin Harris Creative Media
Printed in China by
Hong Kong Graphics & Printing Ltd
for David & Charles
Brunel House   Newton Abbot   Devon

CONTENTS

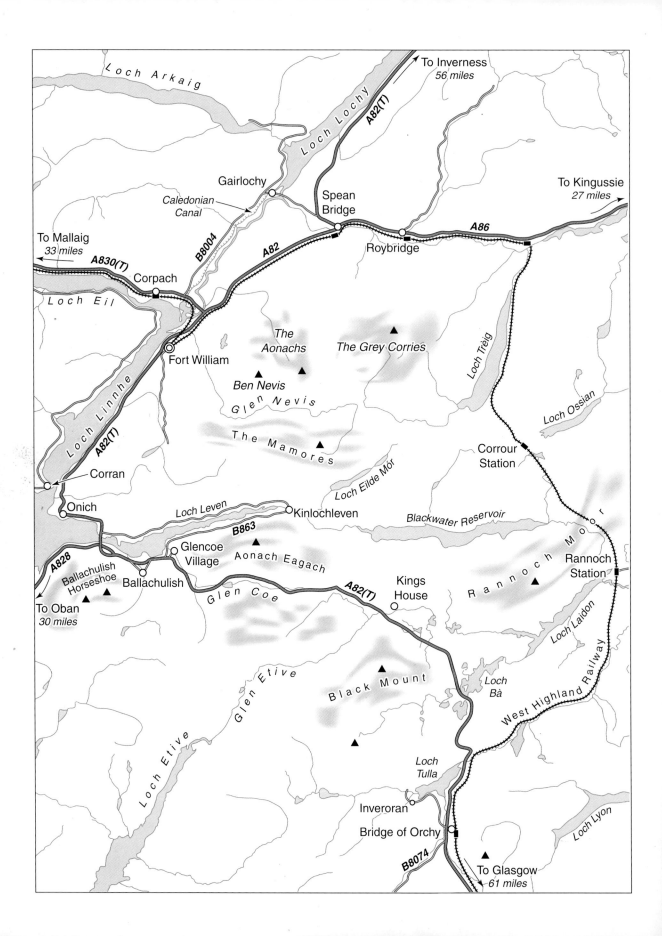

THE BOUNDARIES OF PARADISE

THE PURPOSE OF THIS GUIDE is to introduce the visitor to an extraordinary and charismatic corner of Scotland's Central Highlands, standing proud within the southern bounds of Inverness-shire by the Great Glen within the oft-changed district of Lochaber. Lochaber is not a loch but a West Highland district lying to the east and west of Fort William and the Great Glen. Although the name is alleged to have stemmed from a loch, long since dried up, which originally covered the heart of the district, since the 'forty-five', this is often referred to as the 'Land of Prince Charlie'. From the fifteenth to the nineteenth century, controversy has ebbed and flowed between eminent academics, writers, biographers, cartographers, clan chiefs and various military reports as to the origins of the name; for further information I would recommend the detailed *Romantic Lochaber* by Donald B. MacCulloch (see Bibliography, page 109).

The territory is full of classic mountain architecture on a grand scale, also astonishing engineering achievements and it is rich in colourful history and legend. Here flourish three towering mountain ranges, including Ben Nevis, Britain's highest, and the brooding heights of Glen Coe, softened by a variety of picturesque glens, mysterious moorland and reflective

Glen Nevis to Meall Cumhann, 'narrow-shaped hill', coned Sgùrr a' Bhuic, 'peak of the roebuck' and the heights of Aonach Beag, 'small high ridge'

lochs: a proliferation of Highland integrity *agus solas sìor chaochladh* (and ever-changing light).

This work was to be objective but due to the area's matchless composition I have found it almost impossible to winnow that which exists in nature – the objective view – from what is quintessential or exists merely in the mind – the subjective view. The final result is a guide containing not only objective fact for the discerning, inquiring visitor, but also an invitation to share and compare my subjective impressions of the area, so succinctly portrayed by the old Gaelic phrase, *Tìr nam beann, nan gleann's nan gaisgeach* (land of the bens, the glens and the heroes).

The Gaelic language spread initially during the third and fourth centuries with a small but increasing influx of Irish settlers to Scotland's west coast. By the sixth century, when Columba arrived to spread the gospel, settlements had grown and the language was well on its way to becoming Scotland's oldest tongue in current use. Today its heartlands remain in the West Highlands and Islands with approximately 70,000 Gaelic speakers. Note that the majority of local place names and topographical features are displayed in Gaelic, although in order to assist the non-Gaelic speaker the text includes an English translation immediately following the Gaelic name. This occurs only the first time a place name or phrase in Gaelic is used; subsequent appearances do not carry the English translation.

Covering some 450sq miles (1,165sq km), this lofty land mass rises from sea-level to Ben Nevis' summit, 4,409ft (1,344m), the pinnacle of Britain – the Central Highland's appreciation of the remains of the great mountain mass that soared skywards when the earth was young. Some 400 million years ago ancient metamorphic rocks, schists and intruded granites provided the initial building blocks, later to be fashioned by time and the elements into a high tableland. This was finally split asunder by the abrasive powers of an Ice Age, an erosive process which ended 12,000 years ago when the great ice caps began their final retreat, to unveil the evocative silhouettes that we see today.

Human history dating back to before the second millennium BC – as shown by the solitary standing stone, Clach a' Charra (stone of the monument) at Onich – albeit infinitesimal on the universal time scale, has recorded many violent upheavals and intrusions experienced during the area's physical development. Up to the fourteenth century much of this was not recorded by the Gael save the isolated incident, most being retained in the minds and verse of the bards and story tellers. Paradoxical and no doubt over-simplified, the pressures and the turbulence of nature appear to have been echoed by the hand of man, as is evidenced by the battles of Inverlochy, the massacre of Glencoe, Fort William, the gibbet site by Ballachulish Bridge

Opposite: Ben Nevis – a summer evening's sighting from Corpach Basin

Blackrock Cottage to the cloud-covered Buachaille

and Jacobite memorabilia at High Bridge, the West Highland Museum and the burial grounds of Cille Choireil, Kilmallie and The Craigs.

This guide covers East Lochaber and its surrounds and is divided into five heterogeneous areas, each covered by a separate chapter. As the majority of visitors approach from the south via the A82(T) and/or the West Highland Railway through Bridge of Orchy, it is logical to arrange the chapters in sequence from that particular point of entry. Thus Chapter 1 includes Rannoch Moor; with the A82(T) as lodestar, we progress to Chapter 2 – Glen Coe and Ballachulish – with Chapter 3 serving as a diversion to cover Loch Leven and the Mamores. Chapter 4 describes Loch Linnhe, Fort William and Brae Lochaber, and Chapter 5 the Nevis massif and the Grey Corries. Pausing along the way, as did that great golfer and showman Walter Hagen 'to smell the roses', we tread the ways of those who passed before – clansmen, soldiers, fugitives, pilgrims, drovers and 'caterans' (reivers) – pausing to listen to legend, folklore and the curlew's cry, to indulge in that greatest of British pastimes, 'the weather', and finally to immerse oneself in mountain, moorland and loch, and reflect on tales of great, and at times dark, deeds.

The ferry to and from Ardgour crosses Corran Narrows

Picturesque Rannoch Station on the West Highland Line basking in autumn sunlight

GETTING THERE

UNLIKE MANY HIGHLAND DISTRICTS, good trunk and 'A' roads provide vehicle-friendly access to the perimeter and tempting sightings of what lies ahead, in particular along the northern and southern approaches of the A82(T) – though often to the alarm of the passengers! The A82(T) from Glasgow, fed at Crianlarich by the Edinburgh traffic off the A84(T) and the A85(T), links with the A828(T) Oban to Ballachulish road, to fringe the area's southern and western perimeter. Passing though Glen Coe and Fort William, the A86 Spean Bridge to Newtonmore and Kingussie road provides access to the short northern boundary. For those fortunate to travel from Inverness, serviced by its Highland airport and east coast main-line railway, there is the inviting prospect of a south-west journey through the Great Glen to Fort William, either by boat on the lochs of Ness, Oich and Lochy linked by the Caledonian Canal, or by road alongside the lochs via the A82(T) to Spean Bridge and Fort William.

Internal roads, some just single track with passing places, are limited to a few tarmac ribbons that tentatively probe the hinterland never to emerge at the other side. The B863 cautiously encircles Loch Leven, and there are four unclassified roads: two of these lead from Fort William to Lundavra and Glen Nevis, and the most recent branches off the A82(T) by Torlundy to the Nevis Range Gondola station for Aonach Mòr's skiing,

Eilean Munde, burial island of the MacDonalds of Glencoe

cycling and walking complex. Such is the terrain that even that road-engineering genius Thomas Telford, dubbed by Robert Southey 'The Colossus of Roads', wrote in 1811 'The Road up Glencoe, though preferable to the Devil's Staircase, is one of the most rugged in the Highlands'.

In 1894 Stephenson's successors built the West Highland Railway – surely Britain's most scenic – from Glasgow to Fort William and beyond, over the hazardous blanket bog of Rannoch Moor, and it was they who perhaps provided the finest of scenic approaches into the area, from which all are able to appreciate what lies ahead. 'There are many ways of seeing landscape, and none more vivid, in spite of the canting dilettanti, than from a railway train.' These words of Robert Louis Stevenson ring as true today as when they were first penned to describe this not-to-be-missed journey.

PEOPLE AND PLACES

SETTLEMENTS OF ANY SIZE are few and are located on the perimeter, with the exception of Kinlochleven. Fort William, the fort of 1690, is a name that even today sticks in the thrapple of many Highlanders who refer to it as *An Gearasdan Dubh Inbhir-Lòchaidh* ('The Black Garrison of

Inverlochy'). Habitation grew around it, and after three centuries and three discarded names, the enlarged township of 4,000 and what remains of the fort, is still called Fort William. It is proud to be Lochaber district's administrative capital: since 1996 the district shelters beneath the administrative umbrella of Highland Council. Today, bilingual road signs welcome us to An Gearasdan (The Garrison), accessed by rail, road and sea, a friendly, bustling four-seasons holiday centre with much of interest, including a fine museum and helpful library, attracting thousands of seasonal visitors. Its adjacent villages, each with tales to tell, are fringed by aluminium works, hydroelectric schemes, quarries, pulp and paper mills and the Ben Nevis distillery, plus the eight locks of Neptune's Staircase and the western basin of the great Caledonian Canal at Corpach. Several centuries past, Glencoe village and Ballachulish thrived on the Ballachulish slate industry; today they and their surrounds still retain their character. Seldom visited Kinlochleven depends entirely on Alcan's hydroelectric scheme and aluminium smelter – the world's smallest and longest operating smelter – and the through traffic of West Highland wayfarers. At the time of writing this guide, however, the cloud of closure hangs heavy over the aluminium smelter. Spean Bridge and Roy Bridge, north of Fort William, support an agricultural and forest community and benefit from the tourist trade.

Kinlochleven turbines, Alcan's hydro-electric power house

This is a unique, ever-changing landscape where time is not only measured by the seasonal cycle but also daily, and where climatic changes – at times petulant and dreich and on occasions, at height, downright vicious – present canvases of striking light and subtle shades, with displays of natural artistry that cannot fail to excite all who pass this way. The mountains may be construed as mammoth sculptures, exhibiting as they do rock of all classes and colour. There is a matchless moor, and glens fine in character and form, and also an abundance of probing sea-lochs, reflective lochs, man-made reservoirs, frothy rivers, waterfalls and tumbling *allt* (burns). Add to this an ever-changing light and the seasons' winds, a fine mix of indigenous wildlife including small stands of the Old Caledonian Forest, a visible abundance of colourful, and at times bloody history, and the visible and working engineering achievements of man – and you have Lochaber.

The tranquil Abhainn Shira reflects the twin arches of Victoria Bridge

Opposite: Allt Lairig Eilde, 'burn of the pass of the hind', tumbles downwards

In recent years the film-makers have done much to promote Lochaber, and in particular Glen Nevis and above Kinlochleven, largely with the films *Braveheart* and *Rob Roy*; in fact they have been attracting so many visitors to the 'set' it has been whispered around the Fort that the area is to be renamed *Gleann ceallaloid* (celluloid glen). A forest car park in Glen Nevis now bears the name 'Braveheart'.

This is a land as proud as its sons and daughters, that revels in the splendour of its isolation – except perhaps in the vicinity of Fort William, on the mountain/pony track to the Ben's summit, and several roadside honey-pots during July and August – but even here, solitude is but a short walk away. It is a land with much to do and even more to see, one that will appeal to all, whether rock climber, mountaineer, hill walker,

Above: Ben Nevis (Gaelic compound word Beinn-neimh-bhathais) 'mountain with its head in the clouds', lit by a summer storm

Opposite: Lochs, Leven and Linnhe, to Ardgour, from the summit rocks of The Pap

long-distance walker, loch-side rambler, historian, artist, photographer, fisherman, sailor, cyclist, skier, shinty fan, whisky taster, train spotter or 'Ben runner'. It is a land that will satisfy all the 'ologists and lovers of the countryside, including those who come simply to admire and absorb its matchless surroundings. Should Scotland ever see the advent of National Parks this area would undoubtedly become one of the first.

Stewardship of the environment, in particular of wilderness areas such as those included, is an emotive subject. As situations vary within the guide I feel the following extract from 'A Concordat on Access' as detailed in *Heading for the Scottish Hills* compiled by The Mountaineering Council of Scotland and The Scottish Landowners' Federation, would be most appropriate: 'There is a long-standing tradition of access to hill land in Scotland, cherished by those who use the hills and long accepted by landowners and managers where this freedom is exercised with responsibility.' Details of access and seasonal restrictions are given in the relevant chapters and under Useful Information, page 109, for the benefit of the ever-increasing numbers of visitors who come to enjoy the area, for whatever reason.

There may be occasions when the area's scenic tapestry is hidden in cloud, and times when its heritage has been misted over by tartan-tinted romanticism, yet when both have been burnt off or blown away, what remains is, in the words of the 'Glasgow Boys': 'Dead brilliant, so it is!'

Fàilte – welcome.

1 RANNOCH MOOR AND BEYOND

East and West, and northward sweeping,
Limitless the mountain plain,
Like a vast low-heaving ocean,
Girdled by its mountain chain.

The Moor of Rannoch
John Campbell Shairp

RANNOCH MOOR, ONCE TREE CLAD and roamed by bear, beaver, boar and wolf, is to me an intriguing, magical place whilst remaining something of a mystery, hazed in hearsay and uncertainty.

Purists package it as 56sq miles (145sq km) bound in triangular shape within the high ground east from Beinn a'Chrulaiste (rocky hill) to Lochan a'Chlaidheimh (little loch of the sword) north of Rannoch Station; the West Highland Railway to Bridge of Orchy, then with the A82(T) to Beinn a'Chrulaiste. However, I have extended Rannoch Moor to include Blackwater Moor in which Loch Ossian (Gaelic, loch *Oisein,* meaning loch of Ossian – the Fingalian bard), Corrour Station (Gaelic, *Coire Bhobhar,* meaning watery corrie) and the Blackwater hills link through Blackwater Reservoir to Black Corries Lodge and Kingshouse. The western margins are delineated by the northern fringes of Black Mount,

Above: West beyond Rannoch Moor into the jaws of Glen Coe
Left: Meall a' Bhùiridh mirrored in Lochan na h-Achlaise

North-east over the glacial mounds surrounding Lochan na h-Achlaise

south to Bridge of Orchy. The whole, 'girdled by its mountain chain', clockwise W-N-E from Bridge of Orchy, includes the spectacular ranges of Black Mount, Glen Coe, the Mamores and the Grampians from Beinn na Lap (hill of the mire) to Beinn Dòrain (hill of the otter).

Within these bounds, a haven for fleeing Jacobites, lies a blanket bog of water, peat and glacial debris on and around the 1,000ft (305m) contour, covering a vast saucer of rippled, rolling, impervious granite, formed under the earth's surface by the action of extreme heat erupting through the overlying crust during the Old Red Sandstone Period, 400–500 million years ago. Some 20,000 years ago, relatively recent in geological time, the area was scoured by an enormous glacier which left a landscape of scattered erratics, glacial mounds and rock basins. Folklore however offers a more romantic tale, suggesting the Formorians (Gaelic, *famhair*, meaning giant), a race of rumbustious rock-throwers who spent their days bombarding all and sundry, were responsible for this erratic spread.

Silvery skeleton of the Caledonian Forest risen from the peat

Although little grows above knee height due to deforestation and an increasing red deer population, isolated clusters of stunted rowan, silver birch, pine and bog myrtle inhabit the islands of the lochs. Centuries ago an open mix of indigenous Scots pine, oak, birch and alder, the 'Great Wood of Caledon', thrived on this high water table, providing shelter, grazing and energy for its plentiful wildlife. Alas, widespread clearances, particularly between AD800–1100 and 1400–1700, by charcoal burners, the industrial revolution and eighteenth-century naval expansion, signalled the 'Woods' demise. Today a handful of remnants remain, at Doire Darach (oak grove), Loch Tulla (loch of hillocks) and Crannach (full of trees) east above Water of Tulla, but little else, save a scattering of silvered-root skeletons and severed trunks in bible-black peat graves.

A wilderness, a windy waste it may be, but barren it is not for a diversity of wildlife flourishes, confirmed by the plaintive cries borne on the restless winds of moorland life – rutting stag, curlew, duck and plover, in addition to gulls, skylarks, whinchats and the rattle of moor fowl. Saw-toothed gooseanders and red-throated and black-throated divers are also present. Deer, most reliable of weather-forecasters, abound, also the predatory otter. Botanists have a field day on the moor for a profusion of heathers, ling, lichens and mosses, with sphagnum bog-moss the moor's generator, provide interest and colour. Also to be seen are thyme, lady's mantle, orchids, bog-asphodel, water-lily, yellow flag iris, blaeberry, cranberry and allegedly the Rannoch rush.

Insects are legion, with butterflies and dragonflies providing colour, pond skaters, beetles, ants and bees interest and activity, and what would the Highlands be without the all-sucking, all-stinging nasties, the most voracious being the female *meanbh-chuileag* (midge), with horseflies ('clegs') a close second. Both attack the unprepared in warm, windless conditions from May to October. Of the many repellents available I have found Diethyltoluamide ('Diet' for short) to be the most effective. In vogue are fine-meshed head-nets, often seen crowning the heads of outdoor workers. The deciduous bog myrtle (*Myrica gale*), prevalent and versatile, in addition to flavouring beer and controlling intestinal worms, will, when its leaves are crushed and rubbed, repel insects.

Red deer search for food during Easter week

In Gaelic, Rannoch Moor is *Magadan na Noine* (the plain of the moss-land), and few can fail to be moved by its presence. Love this enchanted solitude as I do, or hate it as did Dr John MacCulloch who in 1811 wrote, 'an inconceivable solitude, a dreary and joyless land of bogs', it remains the very antithesis of the chapters that follow. It cannot be ignored and must be crossed.

Entry is through Bridge of Orchy, a tiny community consisting of the Bridge of Orchy hotel, with bunkhouse, a single-arched rubble bridge of 1742, railway station, shop-cum-post office, and several stone cottages. Motorised traffic speeds along the A82(T) Crianlarich to Fort William highway, pedestrians and mountain bikers via the West Highland Way – 95 miles (152km) from Milngavie, Glasgow to Fort William – and last but not least is The West Highland Railway to Fort William, the UK's most picturesque line, through the heart of the moor. Thousands pass through annually, by bus, bike, boot, car and carriage in search of many things, for as a gateway to the Highlands scene it has few equals.

HIGHWAYS

HOW THEN, AND WHY, did man turn his attention to possible passage through this unpopulated watery wilderness? Cattle no doubt influenced the creation of rough tracks, the recurring Gaelic word *bà* (cattle) within Rannoch Moor is a reminder that highland cattle were raised and grazed here. The 'exchange' of stock between Glen Coe and rival Glen Lyon, and later the great highland droves lumbering south to Falkirk's trysts, also made their mark. The main factor however was unquestionably London's need to contain and quell the Jacobite Risings.

Below: The single-arched eighteenth-century Bridge of Orchy

Bottom: Over Loch Tulla from Doire Darach, a remnant of the 'Great Wood of Caledon'

OLD MILITARY ROAD

THE MOOR'S FIRST LINK of substance was a 12-mile (19.2km) section, between Bridge of Orchy and Kingshouse, of Caulfeild's Fort William to Stirling military road. Major William Caulfeild, appointed Inspector of Roads in 1740, was credited with over 800 miles of highland roads. A lavish host and *bon viveur*, he reputedly displayed his engineering skills by hoisting guests, who had indulged well but none too wisely, into their beds with a block and tackle.

Work began in spring 1752 to build road and bridges over the fringes of Black Mount and Rannoch Moor before the onset of winter, under two civilian engineers and twenty-five officers, with 870 men from the Fort William, Perth and Stirling garrisons.

Today the Old Military Road not overlaid by Old Glencoe Road, has deteriorated to an uncertain trod. The military connection is retained by two features north of Bà Bridge below Scotland's largest coire Coireach a' Bà, Drochaid an t-Saighdeir (bridge of the soldier) and Càrn an t-Saighdeir (cairn of the soldier).

OLD GLENCOE ROAD

THIS 'PARLIAMENTARY ROAD', built in the early 1800s, winds its scenic way over the Bridge of Orchy, by Loch Tulla and Doire Darach, to the site of the original

thatched Inveroran Inn by the stone bridge over Allt Orain (burn of songs) and today's Inveroran hotel *circa* 1708, a hostelry that in the 1890s hosted Scottish Mountaineering Club members, who pioneered winter climbing techniques in the great corries of nearby Stob Ghabhar (goat peak). My memories go back to 1957, a welcoming dinner by gas-light, candles upstairs, feather mattresses and, when strolling in the gloamin' through Doire Darach, the midges!

Beinn Dòrain from the Old Glencoe Road

A half mile or so north of Inveroran is Druimliart (back of the field), birth-place (1724) of Duncan Ban MacIntyre, Donachadh Bàn nan Oran (fair-haired Duncan of the songs). This master bard of the countryside, with no reading or writing, confined his work to memory. Working within the shadows of Beinn Dòrain inspired *Moladh Beinn Dòrain* (in praise of Beinn Dòrain). His shrewd observations on the *Great Sheep of the Clearances* are worth noting:

21

Top: Black Mount's great Coire an Easain seen from the east

Above: Abhainn Shira meanders east from Loch Dochard

My blessings with the foxes dwell
For that they hunt the sheep so well,
Ill fa' the sheep, a grey-faced nation;
That swept our hills with desolation.

The road north crosses Victoria Bridge over Abhainn Shira (River Shira) to Forest Lodge, prior to a car park (free) which marks the end of public vehicular traffic. The bridge was named after Queen Victoria, for it was to this corner she came first when searching for a Scottish residence. Beyond Forest Lodge and the colourful rhododendrons, north to Lochan Mhic Pheadair Ruaidhe (small loch of Red Peter's son), the road follows a lower contour than the Old Military Road, beneath Coire an Easain (corrie of the little waterfall) rimmed by Clach Leathad (pronounced 'clachlet' and meaning declining stones). North of Bà Cottage, at the highest point 1,454ft (443m), extensive views of the moor unfold. Note, above the way there is the small unmarked memorial to Peter Fleming, author, soldier and traveller.

Ahead tower the White Corries, first explored in 1917 by the Ladies' Scottish Mountaineering Club, whose slopes offer long ski-runs, harnessed in 1960 when White Corries Ltd installed a chair-lift to open

Scotland's first commercial skiing facility. Now modernised, the ski-complex provides a complete range of facilities including a ski museum and ski-lifts for a quick and worthwhile summer leg-up to Meall a'Bhùiridh (hill of bellowing stags). Below stands Blackrock Cottage, white walls and black tin roof, once a shepherd's shieling, now the club hut of the Ladies' Scottish Climbing Club, donated by the Marchioness of Breadalbane, the club's first president in 1908. From Blackrock it's but a hop, skip and a jump over the A82(T) to the cluster of Kings House Hotel, known simply as Kingshouse.

With the Old Glencoe Road as an alternative to sea journeys from Glasgow to Fort William, came a 'five-in-hand' coach service in 1834 operating from mid-June to mid-October. Loch Lomond was traversed by steamer, a pleasant and comfortable interlude prior to the rigours of Rannoch Moor and Glen Coe. The inns of Inveroran and Kings House benefited greatly, and an increasing flow of touring literati and the chattering classes donated a crop of comments that may interest readers, if not yesterday's inn-keepers.

Above: The West Highland Way looks closely into Coire an Easain

Below: June's rhododendrons colour the old drove road above Loch Tulla

STANCES

To guard against loss of weight, drovers strove to provide their charges with regular food, drink and rest, stopping overnight at well-watered pastures known as 'stances', normally spaced 10–12 miles (16–19km) apart. Local stances were sited at Spean Bridge, Blarmachfoldach, Glen Kiachnish, Kinlochleven, North and South Ballachulish, Altnafeadh, Kingshouse, Inveroran and Bridge of Orchy.

Prior to the 1850s, stances were mostly free although ownership changes and the Enclosure's Acts altered things, especially if whisky shops or inns fringed the stance. For an overnight stance at Inveroran, Lord Breadalbane is said to have levied a charge of 1s 6d for every 20 cattle or 200 sheep. At its peak up to 7,000 sheep and 10,000 cattle passed by Inveroran annually!

DROVERS

These were plaid-clad and often bare-footed, who on the hoof rested with their cattle, immune to the vagaries of a Highland night. Their diet of oatmeal, onions and milk also fed their collies. During periods of cold 'a drover's black-pudding' was concocted by adding cattle's blood to oatmeal and onions. For further information I would recommend A. R. B. Haldane's The Drove Roads of Scotland *(see Bibliography, page 110).*

Today these old ways are
(continued)

INVERORAN

ALTHOUGH DESCRIBED by Dorothy Wordsworth in 1803, as 'a jewel in the desert', the food was not to her liking, 'the butter not eatable, the barley cakes fusty'. Robert Southey, accompanying Thomas Telford, noted it was pleasing that Lord Breadalbane was replacing, 'the wretched hovel' with a new building.

KINGSHOUSE

ORIGINALLY MILITARY BILLETS, Kingshouses were basic inns situated on King's Highways, many of which did not enjoy the best of reputations. Poor Miss Wordsworth again noted it was, 'As dirty as a house after a sale on a rainy day', and in 1802 James Donaldson said it had, 'More the appearance of a hogsty as an Inn'. An anonymous nineteenth-century traveller declared it, 'The worst inn in Scotland', a reputation that ran into the twentieth century when J. H. B. Bell, eminent Scottish mountaineer, claimed, 'From one's bedroom one could smell the bacon frying through a hole in the floor'.

Charles Dickens, in his tour of 1841, did however enjoy a repast at Kingshouse of, 'kippered salmon, broil fowl, hot mutton, ham, poached eggs, pancakes, oatcakes, wheaten bread, butter, bottled porter, hot water, lump sugar and whisky': a supper that apparently accompanied him into Glen Coe, which he described thus – 'such haunts as you might imagine yourself wandering in, in the very height and madness of a fever'.

DROVE ROADS

THE PRECEDING ROADS, and their attendant inns, are best remembered not as passage for booted redcoats or five-in-hand coaches but as main-line drove roads, along which flowed bovine ribbons of highland cattle (kyloe), their drovers and snappy collie dogs. Scotland's western Highlands and Islands produced fine black cattle, while the industrial heartlands of Scotland and England provided an increasing demand, and as the supply could walk to meet the demand, business thrived.

And so they arrived in Lochaber, from May 'til September, to join the landward droves to the Trysts (livestock markets) of Falkirk and Crieff. The River Spean, liable to seasonal spates during the droving times, was a hazard greatly alleviated by General Wade's High Bridge, which allowed a three-ways funnel through Lochaber to link again at Kingshouse and onward to Inveroran and Bridge of Orchy.

THE NEW ROAD – A82(T)

WITH THE 1930s came the A82: a road, not without its detractors, of distant horizons surging majestically north through Bridge of Orchy, rounding Loch Tulla and crossing the Water of Tulla on the first of several distinctive arched suspension bridges, to rise and fall north-west through a scatter of blue-tinged, isle-strewn lochs. Picturesque and reputedly full of game fish, are Lochan na h-Achlaise (small loch of the hollow), Loch

pounded by thousands – 50,000 per year was quoted – of long-distance walkers, treading the West Highland Way over Rannoch Moor from Bridge of Orchy via Inveroran (hotel, camping) to Kings House (hotel, camping), en route to its Fort William terminus.

Whilst compiling this guide this hugely popular path was awarded a £500,000 lottery grant for pathway maintenance and restructuring.

Below left: The towering peak of Black Mount's Stob Ghabhar from Lochan na h-Achlaise

Below: A distinctive bridge of the A82(T) approaches the guardians of Glen Coe

Buidhe (yellow loch), Loch Bà and Lochan na Stainge (small loch of mountain ditches), revealing much of J. C. Shairp's 'the mountain plain girdled by its mountain chain'. Black Mount's elegant dished wedges of Stob Ghabhar, Sròn na Giubhas (nose of the firs), Clach Leathad and Meall a'Bhùiridh catch the eye, whilst over the moor a platoon of Mamore peaks pierce the horizon.

Rising on the broom-lined way to the summit of the moor at 1,141ft (348m), the road sweeps onwards, as if magnet drawn, to the unmistakable wrinkled guardians of Glen Coe. North of the highway below the hump of Beinn a'Chrulaiste nestles Kingshouse Hotel, providing facilities to suit a variety of customers. In addition to the seasonal armadas of tourist coaches, the A82(T) over Rannoch Moor is serviced all year round by long distance and local service buses.

THE WEST HIGHLAND RAILWAY

FROM THE MID-1800s to the century's end the Highlands were alive with railway mania. Grandiose schemes were legion and as often as not farcical, 'a tunnel through the centre of Ben Nevis' or 'a line to the summit', etc. One proposal however did mature, despite the objection, 'the Deer will not like it'. The West Highland Railway, started in 1889 from Glasgow to Fort William and later Mallaig (although not without a wagon-load of financial, constructional and operational troubles), was completed in 1894 and continues today, the most romantic and picturesque of routes.

The West Highland's audacious 30-mile (48km) traverse of Rannoch Moor made international railway history. Travelling roughly along the same lines as Telford's 1811 rejected road project, it provides a swashbuckling journey that restores lost youth. Saturday 11 August 1894, 8.15am – a day of pomp, ceremony and bagpipes – marked the inaugural journey from Glasgow's Queen Street station to Fort William.

From Bridge of Orchy the line chugs north-east passing the remains of Achallader tower, a Campbell stronghold, through the indigenous woods of Crannach, to reach Gorton Crossing below Learg Mheuran (the robbers' pass), an ancient way from Glen Lyon to Glen Coe. Rannoch Station, built in the style of Swiss chalets with post office and cheery tea room and adjacent to the Moor of Rannoch Hotel, cottages, a road terminus and a waiting post-bus, is soon reached and left via the steel and granite of Rannoch Viaduct, at 684ft (208m) the longest on the line.

Mr Renton's sculptured head adorns the northern platform of Rannoch Station

Mysterious Loch Ossian to Ben Alder's snow

Of all the engineering triumphs in The West Highland saga the greatest was to stabilise the quaking, bottomless moor. Engineer Aird followed Stephenson, the doyen of railways, by 'floating' the line on rafts of heather and brushwood. Ditches were dug, cross-drains cut, turves and scrub laid and as they sank more were added. When supplies ran short, for the moor devoured materials and money, ash and spoil were shipped in. Financed from the private fortune of Mr Renton, a West Highland Director, this extra ballast, and the dry summer of 1893, saved the day. A commemoration by the railway navvies of their sculptured head of Mr Renton still stands on Rannoch Station.

The 7-mile (11km) ascent from Rannoch to Corrour Halt, over Scotland's Central Watershed, passes Lochan a'Chlaidheimh a mile or so north of Rannoch Station. This is an unpretentious lochan with a fine tale to tell, of how Sir Ewan Cameron of Locheil, aided by Gormshùil Mhòr (great blue-eyed one) the witch of Moy, triumphed over the Earl of Atholl in an ownership dispute concerning the grazing lands of Beinn a'Bhric (hill of the trout) and Black Water. Outwitted and outflanked Atholl hurled his claymore into the dark waters, naming it Lochan a'Chlaidheimh – and should you doubt this tale, take note that in 1812 a rusting claymore was recovered from the lochan by a young 'herd and taken to Dr Thomas Ross of Fort William, who declared it the sword of Atholl. It was returned with

27

Phantom Station

Corrour Station, built as a passing place, is possibly the most remote in the land – ticket clerks have denied it exists. Originally a private halt for Corrour estates, it did not appear on public timetables until September 1934. Estate guests were transported by pony and trap 1 mile (1.6km) east to a small wooden boathouse (now a twenty-bunk Scottish Youth Hostel) at the head of picturesque Loch Ossian and then by steam yacht to Corrour Lodge. Today's hostel, a haven for seekers of solitude, entertains eight red deer – 'pets' said a stalker – whose leader 'Windswept' regularly searches for left-overs, devouring everything from bananas to Mars Bars.

The station buildings, including the signal box, have been converted into an all-year bunkhouse accommodating fourteen, with recent additions of shop and café by Station House over the line. Isolated it may be, but from this hub, tracks and paths radiate to Loch Ossian and Rannoch, Loch Trèig and beyond to Blackwater Dam, Kinlochleven, Glen Nevis and Spean Bridge. In the early 1900s job-seeking navvies, regardless of conditions, de-trained at Corrour and legged the 15 or so miles (24km) over the moor to Kinlochleven. Several did not reach their destinations, including a fugitive from Glasgow justice – traced to Corrour, a search of the moor revealed not just his body but the remains of three more.

due respect to the lochan and in the words of Seton Gordon 'its trusty blade turned to glowing bronze in the sunlight, then like Excalibur, it sank for ever from sight'.

As Corrour approaches, at 1,348ft (411m) the highest point on the line, several old railway properties are passed at Lubnaclach (bend of the stone) prior to Loch na Sgeallaig (loch of wild mustard). To the west the sweeping ridges of the Blackwater Hills manifest themselves in Leum Uilleim (William's leap) and Beinn a'Bhric, said to be haunted by the Beinn a'Bhric witch masquerading as a hen or cat.

From Corrour, our railway traverse of the moor ends with a descent of 1,347ft (411m) in 28 miles (45km) to Fort William, but not before the tale of *The Ghost* is told; a legendary night-time freight that personified the unique character of The West Highland Railway.

Dawn was breaking as *The Ghost* puffed into Corrour, slowing to collect the 'tablet' at the station. Once collected the driver gave her full steam ahead, causing a whiplash on the rear-end wagon couplings which detached the brake van – complete with sleeping guard!

The train was now over the summit – not so the brake van which teetered to a stop, paused momentarily and then rolled back with increasing momentum in the direction of Rannoch Station, on what turned out to be a 25-mile (40km) excursion. Railway rules state 'runaways are to be de-railed', but such was this runaway's speed that derailment could have proved fatal for the guard so Rannoch's signalman let her go. As did Gorton's, for now the brake van was running at 35mph (56kmph), and accelerating, to Bridge of Orchy.

Beyond Bridge of Orchy the line ascends, and if the van was still on the tracks through his station the stationmaster judged it would be halted by the incline. It was and it did, two miles away. He found the van silent and stationary. Opening up he wakened the slumbering guard, resulting in the following dialogue recounted by John Thomas in his definitive *The West Highland Railway.*

'Do you know where you are?'
'No,' admitted the guard, looking around.
'You're at Bridge of Orchy,' said the stationmaster.
'Ach, don't be daft we were there two hours ago.'
'Well, well,' retorted the stationmaster, 'you're back again!'

Walks

RANNOCH MOOR provides the outdoor enthusiast with few prepared waymarked paths. What it does provide are the old ways, tracks and trods that wend through hag and heather, offering adventurous days of wild scenery, solitude and satisfaction. There are however others on the moor to consider when setting out on foot.

Overall the numbers of *Cervus elaphus*, the indigenous red deer, have

increased dramatically, above the sustainable level forecast, to the detriment of agriculture, forestry and the deer itself, as culling for venison has not been successful in reducing herd numbers.

The sandy shores of Loch Bà south to Beinn Achaladair

Hinds and stags live apart, coming together for the rutting (mating) season in September and October, a time of bellowing and posturing. Antlers, the status symbol of the Monarch of the Glen, are cast in March and calves are born in late May and June.

Stalking and shooting red deer stags over Lochaber and Rannoch Moor is from 1 July to 20 October, for hinds from 21 October to 15 February, with mid-August to mid-October the most active time. During these periods access may be restricted on Blackmount, Rannoch Deer Management, Black Corries, Killiechonate and Mamore and Corrour estate's land, apart from designated, definitive paths and tracks. Inquire from the appropriate estate office or estate stalker regarding the viability of proposed off-track routes. Estate contacts and telephone numbers are included in Useful Information on pages 108–9.

Inexperienced walkers venturing onto the moor should consider well the cautionary tale of seven ill-prepared businessmen with railway interests who journeyed over the moorland wastes from Inverlair bound for Inveroran in January 1889. It was a foolhardy journey of avoidable disasters through wind-driven sleet for this umbrella-carrying, overweight and non-too-robust gathering who refused over-night shelter on the moor. Five had to be rescued, exhausted and disorientated, by shepherds from Gorton cottage. All survived, but just in time, for the following night Rannoch Moor was buried beneath drifting snow.

Three paths radiate from Rannoch Station. Two, each around 13 miles (21km), are available for dedicated 'bog-hoppers' when visibility is good and underfoot is firm. They share the wooded north shore of Loch Laidon (broad loch), beyond Tigh-na Cruaiche (house on the pinnacle) to the Tayside-Highland Boundary where they split – one on a moorland track to Kingshouse, the second via Tom Dubh-mòr (big black knoll) along Loch Bà's indented western shoreline to the A82(T) at GR 308497. Both routes can be difficult, requiring more attention to map and compass than the aid of the moor's 'bogles' – mysterious guides who assist misplaced souls. An Duine Mòr (the great man) is a kindly but silent spectre, the other, An Duine Eagalach (the fierce-some man), is also silent but chillingly evil. Several documented encounters dating from 1692 are detailed in A. D. Cunningham's delightful *Tales of Rannoch* in which he ponders if the encounters were of the alcoholic kind fuelled in the Moor of Rannoch Hotel and Kingshouse.

Top: Loch Ossian's old boathouse, now a Scottish Youth Hostel of character

Above: Silent sightless ruins of Corrour Old Lodge

The third walk, from Rannoch Station east, provides extensive views of unblemished harmony beyond Blackwater Reservoir to Glencoe's silhouetted skyline, travelling a contouring well-defined way on an old drove road known as 'the Road to the Isles', signposted Fort William by Corrour. It passes *en route* the conspicuous yet solitary ruins of Corrour Old Lodge, windowless on a grassed-over mound, which was many years ago a sanatorium for Glaswegian and local patients. Ahead are the pier and Youth Hostel at Loch Ossian, a loch that can be circumnavigated on estate tracks for seven ethereal miles (11.2km) prior to Corrour.

From Corrour there are the old ways, via Allt a' Chamabhreac (one-eyed trout burn) to Loch Trèig's dark shoreline and the mouth of Gleann Iolairean (glen of eagles) between Sròn nan Gall (nose of the strangers) and Garbh Chnapan (rough hillock). These are ancient routes, trudged by broken soldiery from the 1431 and 1645 battles of Inverlochy, and hurrying caterans treading the Thieves Road from Lochaber to Badenoch.

Beyond the mouth of Gleann Iolairean lies Greaguaineach (green rock) Lodge, gateway to Lairig Leacach (slabby pass) leading into the area covered by Chapter 4, or with Abhain Rath to Glen Nevis into terrain described in Chapter 5.

Passage along an old drove route through Gleann Iolairean to Loch Chiarain (Ciaran's Loch), between the crags of Meall a'Bhainne (hill of milk) and the backside of Beinn a'Bhric, is a solitudinous squeeze south-west with Allt an Inbhir (burn of the confluence), prior to Blackwater Reservoir's shoreline and River Leven's tumbling frothy waters.

2 GLEN COE – THE ENIGMATIC GLEN

horas non humero nisi serenas – I number non but shining hours

GLEN COE, GLEN CONA, Gleann Comhann, Glen of Weeping, Glen of Sorrows, Valley of the Shadow of Death – Scotland's most publicised and stigmatised glen has many names. Deep, steep and rent asunder from east to west as if by the frenzied hand of a primordial axe-man, it lies amidst some of the most imposing and deeply disturbed hills in the West Highlands. Awash with myth and legend and celebrated in verse and song, a landscape that is magnificent but with little mercy, it remains a Mecca for mountaineers, historians, geologists, artists, photographers and tourists.

Glen Coe and Ballachulish embrace four distinct examples of Highlands' format: the glen west from the unmistakable lived-in face of Stob Dearg (red peak), bastion of Buachaille Etive Mòr (great shepherd of Etive) to Glencoe village and Loch Leven; the great corral of

The dark mass of Bidean nam Bian and its buttressed escarpments viewed from Stob Mhic Mhartuin

31

mountains towering south of the glen, host to some of Scotland's finest rock and ice climbs; the daunting northern switchback of Aonach Eagach (notched ridge) between Glen Coe and Loch Leven, and finally Strathcoe and the slate settlement of Ballachulish dominated by the Ballachulish Horseshoe – Beinn a' B'heithir (hill of the thunderbolt). Would that I had the Gaelic, a language with at least forty-four words pertaining to the mountain form, in order to pay due homage to this Highlands galaxy.

Half measures are alien to Glen Coe, as its geological development demonstrates. Three sides of the glen are clad with the contorted rock of

Endless rock and ridge of North Glencoe, including Aonach Eagach, viewed from the Mamores

Dalradian limestones, quartzite, schists and slate – the last is visible in Ballachulish's slate quarries. Also present is evidence of continuous vulcanism, 400 million years ago, in a profusion of layered rhyolite (Stob Dearg on the Buachaille) and andesite lavas thousands of feet thick, layers that subsided into the underground inferno via a distinct encircling fault-line – Clachaig (stony) gully is an example. The intruding magma gave rise not only to the granite basin of neighbouring Rannoch Moor, but also to many of the mountains that grace the glen. Similar rock formations can be found in Greenland, confirming that prior to the Atlantic Rift the land masses were as one. Subsequent glaciation scoured out the softer base rocks to leave a gallery of sculptured truncated spurs and hanging corries of harder material, such as Stob Dearg, Bidean nam Bian and the Three Sisters.

Much has been and will continue to be recorded about this enigmatic glen, a great deal through the pen and brush of yesterday's romanticists. The historian Macauley wrote, 'In the Gaelic tongue Glen Coe signifies the Glen of Weeping [not so], and in truth that pass is the most dreary and melancholy of all the Scottish passes – the very Valley of the Shadow of Death'. These sentiments were echoed by many literati who hurried through, with Charles Dickens in 1841 commenting, 'Glencoe is perfectly terrible – It resembled a burial ground for a race of giants', and surprisingly Seton Gordon in 1935, 'It is a wild and gloomy glen, a fit place for the tragedy – on a bitter February dawn in 1692.'

Others, such as Jim Crawley, Andrew Lang, W. H. Murray and on occasions H. V. Morton speak not only of 'the most celebrated Scottish pass', 'cheerful Glencoe', 'a lesson in humility', but also of fleeting memories of evening's reds and golds of sky and loch. And note the words of MacFarlane's 1600s *Geographical Collections*, 'this countrie is verie profitable, fertill, plenteous of corne, milk, butter, cheese and abundance of fish'.

STEWARDSHIP

As visitors to Glen Coe, we have much to thank the Scottish Mountaineering Club and its 1930s president, Percy Unna, for. After much work and universal fund raising, they bestowed the mountains of Glencoe to the National Trust for Scotland – stewards for the people of Scotland. A letter, dated 23 November 1937 from their president to the chairman and council of the National Trust for Scotland, laid down a series of safeguards concerning the heritage of Glencoe. Known as 'The Unna Rules', they stipulate the land would be held on behalf of the public and preserved for their use, with the Trust undertaking to maintain its primitive condition for all time. Access within the Trust's holdings was to be restricted only by the rigour of the rock face.

Forestry Commission (Forest Enterprise) plantations also provide varied walks and cycleways, as do Glencoe and Dalness estates (National Trust for Scotland). Restrictions are few, being limited to harvesting operations within the forests, the stalking/shooting season on the game estates and controlled culls on others. Details regarding seasonal restrictions are included in the relevant chapters and in Useful Information on pages 108–9.

THE AUTHOR'S GLEN COE

Let the words of Duncan Ban MacIntyre, taken from his masterful In Praise of Beinn Dòrain, *translated by Albert Mackie, speak for me in praise of Glen Coe.*

It's pillared and craggy
And knobbly and shaggy
And pitted and raggy
And rugged and tufted
With dress rough and baggy
Yet pretty and curly:
Its rough little passes
Are lush with tall grasses,
Its richness surpasses
The tamer low country …

The old Glencoe road labours east towards sunlit Buachaille Etive Beag

It matters not what preconceived perceptions one holds, for entry to the Glen is a revelation for visitor and regular traveller alike, whether journeying sedately on foot on the old Glencoe road or surging along the 'new' A82(T) highway.

ROADS

ALTHOUGH ADMIRED BY MANY, the Coe's roads have caused bile to rise in a few craws. Thomas Telford in his 1811 *Report to the Commissioners for Highland Roads and Bridges* stated, 'The Road up Glencoe, though preferable to the Devil's Staircase, is one of the most rugged in the Highlands; the mountains on each side are extremely steep, and from the action of the frost and rain, sheets of rocky fragments are formed, which are successively precipitated to the bottom of the valley'. His assessment was proved correct in 1980, when pouring rain and rapidly melting snow brought boulders crashing down from the Aonach Eagach onto the A82(T), and the site of Achtriochtan (field of three-eighths) clachan, abandoned for that very reason.

New roads also had their detractors. E. A. Baker in *The Highlands* wrote, 'A vast sum was spent, a broad speedway (the A82) has been made following a different line from the old road, cliffs and slopes have been blasted away, leaving scars that half a century will not heal, and now the motor car can rush through Glencoe on top gear'. He concluded with a flourish, 'this new massacre of Glencoe' leaves us 'with a mangled, a ruined Glencoe'.

Altnafeadh (burn of the deer) marks the eastern approaches and the fork of the Glencoe road with the West Highland Way, which follows the Devil's Staircase to Kinlochleven (site of an annual motor-cycle scramble, the dates of which are displayed by Altnafeadh). An entrance dominated by that masterpiece of eruptive sculpture, the furrowed peak of the Buachaille, the gullies, ridges and lofty slabs of which are etched with the names of the early pioneers of rock climbing, Collie, Raeburn, J. H. Bell and the Abraham brothers.

Later, during the depression of the late 1920s, many hiking/climbing enthusiasts moved from Clydeside to live in the hills. Eking out a subsistence living in the Western Highlands the 'Glasgow Boys', as they became known, developed their passion whilst perfecting their climbing techniques, and contributed much to Scottish mountaineering. Buachaille Etive Mòr, although a magnet for mountaineers, must never be underestimated, particularly in winter conditions, as the mountaineering and hill-walking guides in Further Reading (page 109) and the accident statistics will substantiate.

West through the confines of the Pass of Glencoe

Beyond Altnafeadh, as the A82(T) loops south-west over the watershed, the magnitude of the Buachaille and its neighbour Buachaille Etive Beag (little Etive herdsman) or 'wee Buachaille', is revealed. Between them the glacial-trenched Lairig Gartain (pass of the ticks) provides a fine outing, alongside the River Coupal, to the watershed above Dalness in Glen Etive.

Swinging west both 'old' and 'new' roads skirt rush-ridden Locan na Fola (bloody pool), where men fought and died over a cheese, beneath wee Buachaille's bastion Stob nan Cabar (top of the rafters). Ahead, the encroaching spur of Beinn Fhada (long hill) provides the gatehouse for Lairig Eilde (pass of the hinds), a second glaciated trench providing an adventurous trek alongside the tumbling falls of Allt Lairig Eilde, south to Dalness. At the watershed, below Stob Coire Sgreamhach (peak of the scabby corrie) and Stob Dubh (black peak), note the boulder remains of clachan Reamhair (village of travellers). Look out also for the flat Clach an t-Suidhe (stone of the seat), site of shady deals. Clan Reumhair, a sept of Clan Donald, gave clachan Reamhair its name.

It was to this watershed I descended over rock, matgrass and stiff sedge from the summit ridge of Beinn Fhada under a cloudless May sky, having escaped on ridges high and wild from the glen where mountain and man crowd in. *En route* I enjoyed the company of a golden eagle in soaring flight. With obviously more energy than I, but no more *joie de vivre*, it flipped over as it passed me by with not one, but two, victory rolls.

The road wriggles between the Study, from the old Scots 'Stiddie' (smith's anvil), and bubbly River Coe as it enters the Pass of Glencoe, half

Top: From Beinn Fhada's summit ridge to the awesome rock of Gearr Aonach, Aonach Dubh and Aonach Eagach
Above: Terraced rock of Aonach Dubh above River Coe's surging water

Opposite: Bidean nam Bian and the buttresses of Aonach Dubh tower above Achnambeithach

in sunlight, half shadow. To the south tower the bulging buttresses known as the Three Sisters, kept apart by near-naked ravines: from west to east, Aonach Dubh (black ridge), Gearr Aonach (short ridge) and Beinn Fhada, but to mountain enthusiasts 'Faith, Hope and Charity' – with Beinn Fhada as Charity, the greatest of the three. All make up the northern spurs of the ridged and rocky cauldron of Bidean (pronounced bitchen) nam Bian (pinnacle of the bens), unseen from the glen floor, at 3,773ft (1,150m) Glencoe and Argyll's highest. Linked escarpments radiate from its summit, north to Stob Coire nan Lochan (peak of the corrie of the small loch), east to Stob Coire Sgreamhach and north-west to Stob Coire nam Beith (peak of the corrie of the birches). Varied access to these splendid grandstands can be gained from Lairig Eilde, Coire Gabhail (corrie of capture) known also as the Hidden Valley, Coire nan Lochan (corrie of the small loch), or via the Allt Coire nam Beithach.

It is a wonderland offered to all although enjoyed by few, the majority content to gaze from within the touring coach as it twists and turns on A82(T), hotfoot to the Fort. Descending west, above River Coe, passing two rather untidy car parks favoured by motorised visitors and a seasonal piper, the road bisects today's farm and abandoned village of Achtriochtan. Overlooked by the black hole of Ossian's Cave high on the northern face of Aonach Dubh, an unstable climb and unpleasant descent, it was however Glencoe's first recorded climb in 1868 by shepherd Neil Marquis.

Loch Achtriochtan slips by, shallow and reflective, by whose waters the bard Ossian was reputedly born and under whose waters lived a legendary Tarbh-Uisge (water-bull). With the farm of Achnambeithach (field of the birchwood) to the south, the old road acquires a tarmac covering as it crosses the A82(T) for its picturesque sylvan journey north-west, via the Clachaig Inn and bunkhouse and later Glencoe Youth Hostel, to Invercoe, Carnoch and Glencoe village.

The A82(T) continues west, beyond the National Trust Visitor Centre and car park prior to swinging right, south of Achnacon (field of the dogs) and Signal Rock, beneath the hump of Meall Mòr (big hill). Signal Rock, reputed site of the signal for The Massacre (see page 39), can be reached by footpath from the Clachaig and the Visitor Centre. It is from this sweep that access to Gleann Leac na Muidhe (glen of the slab of a churn) can be gained; a sickle-shaped secret in which stood the farm of MacIain of Glencoe who was murdered on that fateful February morning of 1692.

This side glen is a magic place, where solitude and history envelop the visitor. For here, alongside the banks and fluted water-worn rocks of Allt na Muidhe (burn of the churn), overshadowed east by the whale-back of Aonach Dubh a' Ghlinne (black ridge of the glen), fleeing MacDonalds scrambled through February snow to Belach Easan (pass of a waterfall) beneath the craggy and riven rock of Sgor na h-Ulaidh's (peak of treasure) northern face.

THE MASSACRE OF GLENCOE

MANY CLAN CONFLICTS have occurred throughout the Highlands, staining their history with the blood of its people. Some were as barbaric as Glencoe, for example the suffocation by smoke of Eigg's population or the torching of a church congregation of MacKenzies of Urray. Yet none has evoked such bitter memories as the sorrowful event of February 1692, in which the sacrosanct canon of Highland hospitality was held in callous disregard.

In 1691 William of Orange demanded from the Jacobite chiefs an oath of allegiance, to be sworn before 1 January 1692: failure would result in land forfeiture. Lochiel of Clan Cameron, MacDonell of Keppoch and finally MacDonell of Glengarry, swore allegiance within the stated time. MacDonald of Glen Coe, MacIain himself, delayed until the last moment to swear before Colonel Hill, military Governor of Fort William's garrison. Unable to accept MacIain's oath, Hill directed him to a Sheriff at distant Inverary. The severe winter journey, beset by misfortune, resulted in the Campbell Sheriff administering the swearing to Clan Donald on 6 January, six days beyond the deadline.

The reaction of William's minions was predictable, as the letter to Colonel Hill by Dalrymple, The Master of Stair confirms, 'The Earls of Argyle and Breadalbane [reputed to be 'Wise as a serpent, cunning as a fox and slippery as an eel'] were promised that they [the Glencoe MacDonalds] shall have no retreat in their bounds; the passes to Rannoch would be secure'. Confirmation that Glencoe was but a part of overall ethnic cleansing was outlined by The Master of Stair writing to Sir Thomas Livingstone, commander-in-chief, on 7 January, five weeks before the massacre. 'You know that these troops posted at Inverness and Inverlochie will be ordered to take in the house of Invergarie and to destroy entirely the country of Lochaber, Lochiel's

Top left: Loch Achtriochtan cowers beneath the rock of Aonach Eagach
Far left: Stob Coire nan Lochan and Bidean from the flanks of Sgurr nam Fiannaidh
Left: River Coe below Carnoch's beeches

Sculptured rock fashioned by the rushing waters of Allt na Muidhe

Signal Rock reputedly marked the commencement of Glencoe's massacre

Lochiel's lands, Keppoch's, Glengarie's, and Glenco.' A further letter of 30 January found Stair confiding to Livingstone, 'I am glad Glenco did not come in within the time prefixe'.

Glen Coe was disrupted at January's end by the arrival of a 60-year-old tippler, Captain Campbell of Glenlyon, and 120 redcoats of the Earl of Argyll's regiment: a visit viewed with distrust, for had not MacIain's caterans recently cleared Glen Lyon of stock? John, MacIain's elder son, inquired from Glenlyon why a military force had come to Glen Coe, 'Inverlochy barracks is like cried fair' and they had come to Glen Coe for 'bed bite and sup for a week or two'. Alasdair, MacIain's younger son, married to Glenlyon's niece, accepted Campbell's declaration cautiously as Glenlyon's redcoats adopted a policy of 'Hearts and Minds', easing tensions in the clachans at Carnoch, Achnachon, Achtriochtan and Gleann Leac-na Muidhe.

For two weeks the Gaelic-speaking Campbells enjoyed MacDonald hospitality, until a letter from Fort William arrived for Captain Campbell. 'Sir, Persuand to the commander in chief's and my Collonels orders – against the rebells in Glencoe, – by five o'clock to-morrow morning, being Saturday; – It will be most necessary yow secure the avenue to the south, that the old fox, nor non of his cubs, may get away. The orders are, that non be spared from the sword, nor the Government troubled with prisoners.' – Signed James Hamilton. PS 'Please order a guard to secure the Ferry and the boats there' (the 'Ferry' at Ballachulish).

At five the following morning the glen was scarred forever as the violation of Glencoe's MacDonalds began. MacIain, shot at his door, fell dying at his wife's feet. She in turn was robbed of her personal jewellery and 'treted so vilely' she died of her wounds and exposure next day. Thirty-eight of the clan were put to death, and in excess of that number perished in flight over the snow-bound bealachs and mountain ridges, for at the end of the seventeenth century northern Europe was in the grip of the 'little ice age'.

Under Colonel Hamilton 400 redcoats, hours behind schedule due to inefficiency and heavy snow, swept west from Kingshouse burning houses, reiving some 900 cattle, horses and sheep and murdering the one surviving MacDonald left in the glen, an old man of eighty! Hamilton's delay allowed many to evade slaughter by escaping through Lairig Gartain to Etive and Appin, others fled over Rannoch Moor. When news of the massacre was out, Lochiel, Keppoch and Glengarry immediately dispatched any redcoats billeted within their clan lands back to Fort William.

Queen Victoria's passage through Glen Coe moved her to pen, 'let me hope that William knew nothing of it' (ie the 1692 massacre) – an ill-founded hope, if we agree with John Buchan's conclusions in *The Massacre of Glencoe*: 'The burden of the scheme – framed in the latter half of January must rest upon three men, Breadalbane, the Master, and the King. The first

Gleann Leac na Muidhe through which many MacDonalds fled in 1692

has the heaviest share, the last the lightest. In William it was a crime against humanity, in the Master of Stair against his fellow Scots, and in Breadalbane against those who shared with him the blood of the Gael.'

NORTH GLENCOE

WEST FROM THE TOP RUNG of the Devil's Staircase stretches Aonach Eagach, the most familiar of Scotland's great ridges and certainly the most visible. From Sròn a' Choire Odhair-bhig (nose of the dun-coloured corrie) at its eastern terminus, easily reached via the eyrie of Stob Mhic Mhartuin (MacMartin's peak) from whose flanks the River Coe springs to life, this high-level trek strides west for 6½ exhilarating miles (10.5km) via A' Chailleach (The Old Woman), Sròn Gharbh (rough nose), Am Bodach (The Old Man), Meall Dearg (red hill), Stob Coire Leith (peak of the grey corrie), Sgorr nam Fiannaidh (peak of the Fingalians), and finally the optional Pap of Glencoe or Sgorr na Cìche (peak of the breast).

West to The Old Man it is a high, wide and handsome hill walk with revealing views north over Garbh Bheinn (rough hill) to the Mamores and the massif of Nevis. Beyond Am Bodach, the start/finish of what is generally conceived as the Aonach Eagach, its character changes to a high-wire way for the sure-footed and capable mountaineer, an undertaking in winter requiring ice- and snow-climbing experience. Before descending the first chimney, gauge your ability to handle heights (vertigo) and exposure – for there are no escape routes from the ridge – by peering from 'The Old Man's' summit into the almost vertical 2,526ft (770m) couloir to the Dinky Toy cars on the glen floor below.

Descent beyond Sgorr nam Fiannaidh, temptingly close to the Clachaig Inn below, involves a treacherous zigzag alongside the unstable 1,640ft (500m) Clachaig Gully. This gully has claimed lives, one, sadly, the day after the Gully was photographed for this guide. Descend instead to the col below the Pap and then via distinct trods to the dam above Tom Breac (speckled hill), continuing by grassy track (the surrounding pastures/fenced woods are private property) to the old Glencoe road.

Clachaig Gully, slashed deep in Sgorr nam Fiannaidh, above The Clachaig

Opposite: Aonach Eagach's precarious path west, via the summit of Am Bodach

GLENCOE VILLAGE, CARNOCH AND INVERCOE

BEYOND THE WESTERN CONFINES of Glen Coe a widening strath leads to the tranquil scene of white-walled Glencoe village, its surrounding strip-fields and Loch Leven. Strip-field tillage, practised by crofters in the seventeenth and eighteenth centuries on the thin, ill-drained soil of the glen, was based on a system known as lazy beds. The land was worked in strips, the first overturned onto the next strip, which had been 'mucked' with seaweed or animal dung and the seed sown in the sandwich of soil-muck-soil.

Here, in addition to the Glencoe and North Lorn Folk Museum (a rich vein of local information), are shops and a range of accommodation, from hotels to caravan and camp sites (making a total of four in Glen Coe), facilities which indicate that the main activity of this reverse side of the Coe is tourism. Thankfully it is a restrained development, hopefully not to burgeon into a theme park. Nearby, north of Carnoch through stands of landscaped conifers above Invercoe House, there lies one of Glencoe's best kept secrets – a delightful forest walk, the Lochan Trail (with car park). Invercoe House was the seat of Baron Strathcona (valley of Coe). Born in Forres in 1820, he rose from being a clerk in the Hudson Bay Company to High Commissioner for Canada in 1896. The lake and pines were designed to re-create a taste of native Canada for homesick Lady Strathcona, whose ancestors were indigenous North Americans. Climatic differences perhaps hastened their return to Canada.

Carnoch, and the branching B863 to Kinlochleven (see Chapter 3), are left as the A82(T) passes the neat cottages of Tigh-phuirt (house of the seaport) bound for the slate village of Ballachulish. Of interest is the effect the slate quarries had on the two communities after the Massacre. Glencoe and Ballachulish sustained approximately 200 souls, gradually rising in the latter half of the 1700s. By 1871, due to quarry expansion, the population was 1,529 and in subsequent years swelled to 3,000 when the quarries were in full production. Yet within ten years numbers fell to below 1,500 due to a period of reluctant emigration and reduced quarry activity.

The 1791 *Statistical Account* records that 74 families provided 322 workers for quarry work, and each family had a cow and plots for vegetables and paid an annual rent of £2 5s per house, £1 6s per pasture and 15s per plot.

BALLACHULISH

BALLACHULISH (Gaelic, *Baile a' Chaolais,* meaning village of the strait) is not to be confused with South Ballachulish and North Ballachulish 3 miles (4.8km) west.

Slate was first quarried at East Laroch quarry, Ballachulish, in 1693 and West Laroch in 1694. The slate, a grey-blue type of high quality, was

Ballachulish headstones, slate sentinels gazing silently into Loch Leven

worked by 'crews' of four to six quarrymen to whom the rock was con-tracted annually. Each crew was paid a bargained rate for a given number of slates, receiving on average 12s per week per man, although a good 'crew' member could earn £1 per week. Ballachulish slate commanded a premium and was sold per thousand, one slate in each batch marked with the castellated tower trademark of 'THE BALLACHULISH SLATE QUARRIES Co Ltd, ARGYLLSHIRE'. Slates were sized and graded into Duchesses, Countesses, Marchionesses, etc. and Sizeable 14in x 8in and Undersized 10in x 6in, Ballachulish producing mainly the latter two. Slates were sold for roofing, gravestones (engraved headstones adorn the burial ground of St John's, Ballachulish), pavements and soles for drainage tiles, establishing a reputation throughout Britain and the Americas. Production peaked in the 1870s, when 26 million slates were produced annually and shipped from the jetties and staithes at Rhudha na Glas-lice (point of the stone hollow) which is composed of slate quarry rubbish. Production ceased in 1955. Further information is available at Ballachulish Tourist Information Centre slate exhibition.

Jetties of discarded slate at Rudha na Glas-lice are still in use by today's fishermen and pleasure craft

45

The slate promontories, north of East Laroch Quarry and adjacent to the Isles of Glencoe Hotel, today provide anchorage for pleasure craft, access to the Isles of Glencoe, scenic footpaths and a spacious car park. From here spectacular sunsets over Loch Leven to Ardgour's serrated sky-line can be enjoyed.

ISLES OF GLENCOE

EILEAN MUNDE OR MUNDA (St Munn's or Munnu's island), was named after the seventh-century Celtic St Fintan Mundas, whose small church remained in use until 1653. Visits to the island are possible, courtesy of local boatmen, from Rhudha na Glas-lice. Although referred to as The MacDonald Burial Isle, it is in fact a divided burial ground: south-east lies Clan Donald, including MacIain of 1692, north-east rest Camerons of Nether Lochaber, south-west sleep Stewarts of Appin and north-west entomb MacKenzies of Onich and North Ballachulish. Many decorative and descriptive gravestones grace the isle, including that of a young quarry-man, killed while shot firing, on whose head a dove is reputed to have placed a white feather. Another bears the acidulous message:

> *My glass has run*
> *Yours is running*
> *Be warned in time,*
> *Your hour is coming*

Adjacent isles are Eilean nam Faoileag (island of the seagulls), Eilean a' Chomhraidh (island of discussion) where disputes were thrashed out then ratified on Eilean na Bainne (isle of covenant), and Eilean Choinneich (Kenneth's island). Eilean an Dunain (island of the little knoll) floats by the north-east corner of Eilean Choinneich.

Above: May's bluebells grace the grounds of St John's, Ballachulish
Left: Disused slate quarry of East Laroch, beyond Loch Leven and Eilean Munde

Churches are in evidence in and around Glencoe village, the majority being nineteenth century, including St Mary's (Episcopalian), St Muns (Roman Catholic), St Munda (Church of Scotland), United Free Church and at Ballachulish, St John's (Episcopalian). In 1784 the Reverend MacColl, St Mary's, ill-advisedly prayed for the Hanovarian George III during service, prompting kirk members to rise from prayer and protest.

St John's Church and burial ground, a few hundred yards west of Ballachulish overlooking the A82(T) and Loch Leven, presents a pleasing picture in total harmony with its surrounds. Sadly the majority of motorised visitors catch but a fleeting glimpse as they speed by, missing May's bluebell

Right: The decorative headstone of master quarryman Kenneth MacKenzie and his mother
Below: 'Modern' Ballachulish Bridge spans The Narrows
Opposite: The Ballachulish Horseshoe, Beinn a' B'heither, towers above Glencoe village, Ballachulish and Loch Leven

carpet and surrounding rhododendrons alongside the unique slate head-stones. Many, sculptured and engraved by master quarryman Kenneth MacKenzie (1816–1901) of West Laroch, are identified by 'fecit K M' on the reverse of each tombstone. A particularly striking headstone, that of a lady's profile, at the church's north-east corner, marks MacKenzie's mother's grave in which he is also buried.

West from St John's the A828(T) Oban road branches right from the A82(T). For those wishing a speedy departure to North Ballachulish and into Chapter 3, cross the narrows of Loch Leven via the modern steel-gird-ed Ballachulish Bridge *circa* 1975. For a more leisurely departure spiced with interest, take the Oban Road beneath the bridge to park by Ballachulish Hotel overlooking the narrows, Caolas Mhic Phadruig (the narrows of Peter's son), named after a Norseman's son drowned after an abortive rescue from the split rock, Clach Phadruig (Peter's stone), east of the jetty.

Ferries operated at the time of the Massacre, recorded in Glenlyon's final orders, and in droving times cattle tackled Loch Leven's tidal currents by swimming after the lead beast which was towed by the horns by a drover in the rowed ferry. Also of interest, reached by signposted stairs below the bridge, is a memorial on Gallow's Hill, South Ballachulish to James Stewart – 'James of the Glen' – executed by hanging from an iron-plated gibbet on 8 November 1752, as an accessory to the murder of Colin Campbell ('Glenure' – the Red Fox in R. L. Stevenson's *Kidnapped*). Glenure was killed by two shots from the 'Black Gun of Misfortune' and one of four possible weapons is displayed in the West Highland Museum, Fort William. It was a dastardly crime (the hanging, not the murder), a controversial trial and a disputed verdict detailed in fact and fiction.

It is fitting that this chapter's western extremity should be graced by a mountain to match the eastern guardian. Towering above Ballachulish, the Ballachulish Horseshoe, Beinn a' B'heither (hill of the birches) embraces two Munros, Sgorr Dhearg (red peak) and Sgorr Dhònuill (Donald's peak), and a capful of tops. Fine of form, especially when seen from North Ballachulish or Onich, its peaked, knobbly ridges encircle a central basin providing a seat in the gods for those who surmount the walnut-whip peak of Sgorr Dhònuill to gaze in awe to all points of the compass, but especially into Glen Coe.

Over Loch Leven to the western gateway of Glen Coe

3 LOCH LEVEN, KINLOCHLEVEN AND THE MAMORES

All around the ancient mountains sat like brooding witches.
– Naked to the four winds of heaven and all the rains in the world.
Children of the Dead End Patrick MacGill

DISPARATE FEATURES MAKE STRANGE BED-FELLOWS, yet within the compass of Loch Leven, the Mamore Forest and the flooded moorland plateau of Black Water there lies a land of symbiotic partnership in which complete harmony exists between loch, mountain rock and wilderness.

Lying immediately north and far below Glencoe's northern perimeter ridges the two-tone waters of Loch Leven, a tributary loch, ebb and flow with the tides of Loch Linnhe. This delightful loch, 10 miles (16km) long and narrowing from 1 mile (1.6km) wide to approximately 270yd (250m) at its head, squeezes west from Kinlochleven to its confluence beyond North and South Ballachulish and is overlooked on its northern shores by the soaring peaks of the Mamores. An appealing, shallow, tidal loch, rather

From the top step of the Devil's Staircase north over Loch Leven to the Mamores

Beinn na Caillich above Loch Leven

*Loch Leven's mountains framed
in silver*

fiord-like, it was originally an ancient river system running the course of today's River Leven through Blackwater to Loch Rannoch. In recent geological time, a downward westerly tilt of Scotland's coastline caused the sea to flood into many narrow coastal glens. The 'Leven' glen was later modified by the Loch Leven glacier, converting the design from a V shape to a narrow U – an ice movement that was also responsible for the deposition of gravel fans at North Ballachulish and Rhudha Charnuis (Carnus point). There are many viewpoints surrounding the loch that present its attributes to advantage – east above Kinlochleven, or from the West Highland Way by Beinn na Caillich (the old woman – locally A'Chailleach) – but to see the complete canvas in all its splendour, from Kinlochleven to Loch Linnhe and beyond, climb to the grandstand summit of Sgorr na Cìche.

Kinlochleven, an isolated community of 1,000 or so (in 1991) at the head of Loch Leven, evolved from six cottages, three on each side of the River Leven, bursting to life with the advent of the twentieth century, hydroelectricity and aluminium. One of two settlements, the other being North Ballachulish, within this area of few people, Kinlochleven's situation is remote and confined by the shadowy heights to the south. There lies 5 miles (8km) east from Kinlochleven the great reservoir of Blackwater astride the solitude and wilderness bogs of what was Black Water river. It seeps from the east, 8 miles (12.8km) long, restrained at the western end by a massive dam. An ever-present memorial to man's ingenuity and navvies'

endeavour, this extraordinary tank and its surrounding hills, linked by a network of tracks and trods, provides a most rewarding outing, particularly in the glad times of spring or with autumn's coppers, reds and golds.

As this chapter lies at the heart of the guide it is fitting to recall a 1790s local weather report by the perceptive Reverend Alexander Fraser: 'The climate cannot be reckoned unwholesome, for several have lived to an advanced age [six of 102–109 years] yet the air is moist, for the wind blows off the sea nearly two-thirds of the year. This accounts for almost incessant rains which prevail not only here, but in all other places on the West Coast of Scotland.'

Immediately north of Loch Leven and Kinlochleven stands the Mamore Forest. One literal translation of the Gaelic Màm mòr is 'large breast-shaped hill', although such cannot in truth apply to this mountain cluster of rocky summits and steep-faced corries reaching skywards above Loch Leven's northern shore. Running east to west for 7½ miles (12km), this close-knit herd contains no less than eleven peaks over 3,000ft (915m), six named summits exceeding 2,500ft (762m) and five attaining the 'mountain' height of 2,000ft (610m). Each is inexorably linked with its neighbours, with the possible exception of the eastern sentinel, Sgùrr Eilde Mòr (big peak of the hind), by a web of interconnecting ridges. Such classification into 'Munros', 'Corbetts' and 'Donalds' may be considered somewhat

Top: The hump of Sgùrr Eilde Mòr

Above: Blackwater Reservoir and the Mamore range sparkle in January's crystal light

fatuous throughout the Highlands, for all are known, regardless of height, quite simply as 'Hills'. So fine is this elegant range when compared alongside the elite, it is little wonder that its popularity increases.

ROADS AND TRACKS

PRIOR TO THE DEVELOPMENT of aluminium smelting, hydroelectricity and Kinlochleven, the only access to the area was what remained of Caulfeild's Old Military Road and the old drove route, journeying from the Devil's Staircase above Altnafeadh, at Glencoe's eastern portal, north to Loch Leven-head. From here it ascended west and north through Lairig Mòr (big pass) betwixt towering Mamores and the twin humps of Beinn na Caillich and Màm na Gualainn (rounded hill of the shoulders). Note,

prior to swinging north above Allt na Lairige Mòire (burn of the broad pass) at the southern slopes of Meall a Chaorainn (hill of the rowans), the one-time shepherd's shieling, Lairigmòr, from where a rough but scenic path runs south-west to Callert House by Loch Leven. Ahead, within the regimented plantation east of Lochan Lunn da Bhra, Lundavra (the fort in the water), 500ft (152m) above sea-level and home to a mythical water bull, stands a cairn said to mark Clach nan Caimbeulach (stone of the Campbells). It was here that Montrose's victorious troops abandoned their pursuit of Campbells after the 1645 Battle of Inverlochy.

The Old Military Road, now the West Highland Way, to Lairigmòr and Fort William

Once clear of the conifers, the Old Military Road continues its 'uppa-downa' journey north via Blarmachfoldach (field of the hospitable sons) to Fort William (see Chapter 4), in which an explanation is given for why Blarmachfoldach welcomed the New Year on 12 January. The hugely popular West Highland Way, our constant companion from Altnafeadh, leaves the Old Military Road for an impressive, needle-strewn Nevis Forest journey into Glen Nevis and onward to Fort William.

Only one tarmac road, the twentieth-century B863, a little-travelled switchback around Loch Leven, allows motorised access into the area. Its first leg, along Loch Leven's northern shoreline, connected the A82 at North Ballachulish to Kinlochleven, which, before 1922, had been limited to passage by boat of shallow draft or a long, tedious trudge round the unmarked shoreline. The second leg, known as the 'German Road', is above the southern shoreline, connected with Glencoe village and the A82, was built initially by German POWs detained in Kinlochleven's First World War prison camp. When completed it provided a 20-mile (32km) alternative to crossing Ballachulish narrows by ferry – crossings which could be agonisingly slow at the height of the holiday season. Today such frustrations are resolved thanks to the opening, in May 1975, of the metal-girdered Ballachulish Bridge spanning the narrows from South to North Ballachulish. Unfortunately many who surge over the bridge are totally oblivious to Loch Leven and its impressive scenery.

Kinlochleven with Alcan's aluminium smelter and hydroelectric power house

The B863, a designated tourist route, leaves the A82(T) north at Glencoe village to pass Invercoe before swinging right to the lochside below woodlands surrounding Invercoe House. The road above the southern shoreline provides fine views over Loch Leven as it winds east, with Caolasnacon below, today a spacious caravan, camping and canoeing site. Caolas nan Con (the narrows of dogs) had to be dredged, and Allt Glean a'Chaolais (burn of the glen of the narrows), running off the Aonach Eagach, had to be diverted in 1907 to prevent silting, thus allowing boats to pass. Indigenous trees grace hillsides and shoreline, enhancing the continuous views of the Mamores. A strategically placed picnic site is passed above Camas na Muic (bay of pigs), and below is the brooding hulk of Garbh Bheinn, prior to a series of bends heralding Kinlochleven.

KINLOCHLEVEN

Though up may be up and down be down,
Time will make everything even,
And the man who starves at Greenock town
Will fatten at Kinlochleven.
         A Wee Song Patrick MacGill

KINLOCHLEVEN (Gaelic, *Ceann Loch Leamhain*, meaning head of Loch Leven) was a somewhat divided community in its early days. Known as Kinlochmore and Kinlochbeag, the hamlets lay on opposing sides of the River Leven, with the counties of Inverness-shire and Argyll locking their civil horns over whether or not Argyll should administer not half but the entire town. After many heated ruts and much posturing, matters were resolved by returning to the *status quo*. Today, after regional reorganisation, both 'more' and 'beag' – well fitted out with facilities and information regarding travel, accommodation and the aluminium story for the visitor – lie within the jurisdiction of Lochaber District Highland Council as Kinlochleven.

HYDROELECTRICITY AND ALUMINIUM

Top: Pipeline from Loch Eilde Mòr to Blackwater Reservoir

Above: Downtake pipes from the heights above Kinlochleven to the power house

IN 1904 Loch Leven Water and Electric Power Co was formed to develop a factory for aluminium production. Later merging with the British Aluminium Co, they acquired at the turn of the twentieth century water rights options in the area of the Black Water lochans, from the kernel of Rannoch Moor to Kinlochleven heights.

This colossal undertaking, the largest in Europe when built, provided a reservoir within a catchment of 65sq miles (168sq km), gathering the annual rainfall of 82in (208cm) per year. The dam was constructed 1905–9; it measured 300ft (91.5m) long and 80ft (24m) high, providing a storage capacity of 3,930 million cu ft (1,112 million cu m) and a maximum head of water of 925ft (282m). The water supply was supplemented from Lochs Eilde Mòr and Eilde Beag in 1916, by a pipeline built by German POWs from the camp above Kinlochleven. A stone zigzag, constructed and used daily from camp to pipeline, is in use today, providing access to Lochs Eilde Mòr, Eilde Beag, the eastern Mamores, Blackwater Reservoir and beyond to Loch Trèig. So too is the West Highland Way, ascending south-east from Kinlochleven with the six-barrelled downtake pipeline carrying water to the power house. A journey through grove after grove of red-berried rowan reveals ever-changing views of the eastern and southern profiles of the Mamores, and the less familiar though nonetheless appealing aspects of Coire Mhorair (Lord's coire) and Sròn Garbh at the Aonach Eagach's eastern extremity. Leave the West Highland Way at the head of the pipeline, and following a vehicular track alongside the concrete conduit, continue for 3 miles (4.8km) or so through the solitude to the wilderness surrounding Blackwater Dam and its seemingly endless reservoir.

Smelting operations require vast amounts of electric power, and power was generated from water supplied from Blackwater Reservoir via the dam and a manifold pipeline running 4 miles (6.4km) to the generators at Kinlochleven. The power house held eleven 3,200hp hydroelectric sets for aluminium making. The main smelter began production in 1909, although the first metal was produced in 1907 by a temporary smelter, with medallions struck from the first ingots bearing in Gaelic, 'What will water not do, when it made me'.

Aluminium is produced from bauxite, a mineral named after Les Baux, France, where it was discovered in 1821. A two-stage process converts bauxite to aluminium oxide (alumina) which in turn is reduced by electrolysis to pure aluminium. Four tonnes of bauxite yields two tonnes of alumina, and with the aid of 13,000 units of DC electric power and 420kg of anode carbon, produces 1 tonne of aluminium. Kinlochleven's smelter, now Alcan Smelting and Power UK, specialising in high purity and foundry alloy aluminium, which commands a premium, is the world's

More water for the power house from Coire Mhorair Dam

smallest and oldest smelter. Sadly, the threatened closure of this unique plant carries with it the scourge of 100 job losses. Already its former carbon bunkers have been refashioned into industrial units and a Hillwalking and Outdoor Activity Centre. Bunkhouse accommodation, a mountain garden complex and an aluminium smelting interpretative centre are proposed for the future, and the multi-storey building standing above the smelter, originally a hostel for single staff, is now leased to the MOD. Let us hope that sustainable jobs return to Kinlochleven and it does not have to depend entirely on West Highland wayfarers and tourism.

The coming of British Aluminium to the wild and beautiful wilderness surrounding Black Water and the isolated head of Loch Leven turned the surrounding area on its head, generating not only electricity but also the community of Kinlochleven – an operation that required a labour force 2,000–3,000 strong, from the four corners of the kingdom, the majority being Gaelic-speaking Highlanders or Irish navvies.

They existed in temporary wooden shanties, often windowless or doorless, sleeping three to a bunk under one blanket, on the heights east of Kinlochleven. Patrick MacGill, a Kinlochleven navvy himself, in *Children of the Dead End* recounts a descriptive, moving tale of the itinerant navvy's life and times in the bogs and rocks of Blackwater: 'We were the men sent out to fight the spirit of the wastes, rob it of its primeval horrors, and batter down the barriers of its world-old defences.' Manual work in these harsh surroundings, aided only by hand-held tools – crowbar, jumper, hammer, pick and shovel – took its toll, as the small graveyard below Blackwater Dam testifies. Twenty simple headstones, fenced and surrounded by daffodils tended by the Kinlochleven smelter hydro team, one marked 'Not Known', others with names such as Darkey Cunningham, Patrick Ryan, John MacKenzie and Mr Riley, remind us of the hardships

Finished product – aluminium ingots

Navvies' graveyard – poignant reminders below Blackwater Dam

and risks of the navvy's life. MacGill's poignant words add finality: 'A few went there from the last shift with the red muck still on their trousers. Once dead they were buried, and there was an end of them.'

This hard-working community was as wild as its surrounds and as lawless as the prospecting settlements of Klondyke and Eldorado. It was an incredible place of gambling dens and the occasional whisky shop, where the only law enforcers were two policemen, armed with truncheon and revolver, to escort the postman on his round. The opening of the West Highland Railway across Rannoch Moor gave the navvies an alternative although hazardous and ill-advised approach to Kinlochleven, by train to Corrour and a 15-mile (24km) trek west over the wilderness.

Stepped and colourful, the West Highland Way winds through the silver birch of Màm Mòr

The journey with the B863 along the north shore (with car parks, lay-bys and caravan and camping sites) to North Ballachulish, varies from the previous leg as it hugs the waterline beyond Eilean nam Bàn (islet of the women), 1½ miles (2.4km) west of Kinlochleven. Festooned for much of the way with pine and fir, oak and ash, rowan, hazel and wild rose, this bosky shoreline offers occasional sitings of a bobbing grey seal, attracted no doubt by the fish farm by Callert. And as befits this tight, irrigation-advantaged glen, its banks display a variety of mosses, ferns and insidious bracken, amongst which can be seen the seasonal colours of many indigenous wild flowers such as primrose, wood anemone, bluebell, bell heather, yellow iris and foxglove.

Callert House (originally meaning hazel point, but now dark conifer), opposite Invercoe, is of interest. Originally the family seat of Cameron of Callert, it was in the 1600s infected with a fatal plague transmitted from a Spanish merchantman anchored in Loch Leven, killing all but a daughter, Mairi Cameron. Across Loch Leven, from Callert to Ballachulish, are fine views of the Isles of Glencoe, including Eilean Munde (see Chapter 2), and the horseshoe of striking ridges that make Beinn a' B'heither so distinct. An ornate granite mausoleum stands 1½ miles (2.8km) west of Callert House, in which the Camerons of Callert House are at rest.

Continuing west above the indented shoreline lies Bishop's Bay below the large house of Alltshellach. Past residence of the Bishop of Argyll and the Isles and later a military hospital, it is today a walking holiday centre, best remembered by the discovery, in 1880, of an ancient female effigy carved from an alder trunk in the peat moss of Goirtean Frideig (Fridda's little field). First thought to be the Norse goddess Fridda, the effigy with quartzite eyes now rests in Scotland's National Museum in Edinburgh. It is dated around 650BC, linking it to early indigenous inhabitants.

NORTH BALLACHULISH

STANDING AT THE NORTH END of Ballachulish Bridge, neat and tidy on a gravel deposit of glacial outwash known as the Ballachulish Narrows, North Ballachulish (Gaelic, *Baile a' Chaolais*, meaning village of the narrows) marks the meeting of the B863 and the A82(T). The colourful rhododendron and bluebell-lined route from it leads to Onich and Nether Lochaber (see Chapter 4).

THE MAMORES

ALTHOUGH OCCASIONALLY PRESENTED as the easy option when compared with The Ben or Glen Coe's obtruding rock, it must be recognised that the Mamores' high corries, ridges and peaks in adverse weather or under winter conditions must be approached with care and respect. Access to the heights is facilitated by a web of estate and stalker's tracks and paths that probe into the heart of the hills, particularly from Kinlochleven and Caulfeild's Old Military Road to Fort William, known today as the West Highland Way. Access is also possible from Glen Nevis (see details in Chapter 5).

Bell heather flourishing at Camus na Heridhe

The Mamore Forest, a medieval deer-hunting forest up to the mid-1400s, fell within the stewardship of the Keppoch MacDonells when they were transferred to Clan Cameron with the marriage of Alan, Ailean nan Creach (Alan the Cateran) to Mariot, Keppoch's only daughter. They, the surrounds of Loch Leven, and north from Blackwater Reservoir to Brae Lochaber, now fall within Killiechonate and Mamore estates, owned by British Alcan Aluminium plc, and administered by the West Highland Estates Office, Fort William. Mountaineers, walkers and lovers of the great outdoors are welcome, although during the stalking season they are requested to keep to established routes and to contact the estate stalker. Further details are given in Chapter 1 pages 28–9, with contacts and telephone numbers in Useful Information on page 109.

From Kinlochleven, where parking, refreshment and accommodation are at hand, paths radiate in a wide arc east, north and north-west, providing access to the high ridges, corries and summits. Commencing with the easterly outlier, Sgùrr Eilde Mòr, north of Loch Eilde Mòr (big loch of the hinds), a leg-stretching 3¾-mile (6km) walk-in to Coire an Lochain (corrie of the small loch) leads via the brisk southern shoulder to the quartzite-capped, long summit spur. An alternative ascent skirts Loch

Eilde Mòr to the isthmus of Loch Eilde Beag (little loch of the hinds), then north by stalker's way to the north-east ridge. From Loch Eilde Beag the way continues north to Luibeilt (steep rock corner) by Abhainn Rath, leading out of this chapter to access Glen Nevis, Lairig Leacach and Loch Trèig (see Chapter 5), scenic journeys that provide distant views south-east over Blackwater Reservoir.

The two Binneins (sharp peaks), Mòr and Beag (big and little), appear slightly adrift and aloof to the east, as befits Binnein Mòr, the highest Mamore at 3,701ft (1,128m). Approached from Kinlochmore, 'Mòr' requires a 3¾-mile (6km) hike to the south-east ridge, then via a stalker's zigzag north to the top listed as Sgor Eilde Beag, from where a curving ridge connects to Binnein Mòr's unmistakable summit.

Eight 3,000ft (915m) Mamores rise to the west, bonded by interlinking bealachs enabling the enthusiast to visit each summit in a long day's traverse via high, wide (although not entirely) and handsome ridges. For the less energetic these sublime peaks can be enjoyed singly or in small

Autumn colours on Caulfeild's Old Military Road, with Am Bodach beyond

groups. A selection of initial walk-ins allow ascent of Na Gruagaichean (the maidens), either from Kinlochleven north beyond the spectacular falls of the Grey Mare's Tail to link with a stalker's path at the sheep pens, GR 191640, below Rhuigh Breac (speckled base of the mountain), or via the prominent Mamore Lodge, originally a shooting lodge favoured by royalty, now a mountain walker's hotel, north-east to GR 191640, then north into Coire na Bà (coire of the cattle), between scree-clad Leachd na h-Aire (stony promontory), the crags of Sgor an Fhuarain (rocky peak of the well) and the east face of Am Bodach (the old man). The cairned summits of Na Gruagaichean, reached by a series of zigzags east onto the maiden's western ridge allow, on cloud-free days, sightings of The Ben's north-eastern profile.

The graceful snow-clad corries and curves of Binnein Mòr

Overleaf: Binnein Mòr in winter, over Glen Nevis from Meall Cumhann

Am Bodach's coned peak of stones is gained from where the way-marked West Highland Way, ascending through an autumn wonderland of rowan 1½ miles (2.4km) north-west from Kinlochmore, crosses the hurrying Allt Coire na h-Eirghe (burn of the boundary coire). Then north by trod, following the burn's true right bank, to loop onto Am Bodach's western bealach. The final ascent east onto the coned peak is stony and steep. One hot August day, whilst leading a party alongside the tree-lined way bound for the stony peak, we experimented with herbal cures for the Mamore Midge. One member, a herbalist by inclination, recalled, 'the leaf of myrtle is an effective midge repellent'. 'Not so,' a young urbanite piped up later as midge activity increased, 'I've just eaten three leaves and they've had absolutely no effect!' – not realising they should be crushed and applied externally!

Below Am Bodach's peak, a contouring path north links the summit ridges of Stob Coire a Chàirn (peak of the corrie of the cairn), An Garbhanach (the rough ridge) and An Gearanach (the complainer). From this point descent into Glen Nevis is possible via a steep zigzag in Coire Dubh (black corrie), east of An Steall. An alternative high-level adventure utilises the pathway west from Am Bodach, encircling the hanging valley of Coire a' Mhàil (corrie of the rent) to Sgorr an Iubhair (rocky peak of the yew), high gateway to a basket of peaks and ridges including the Devil's Ridge to Sgùrr a'Mhàim (peak of the large rounded hill). At 3,606ft (1,099m) this dominant-domed quartzite peak with many corries, including Coire nan Cnàmh (corrie of the cud), was used centuries ago as a high summer pasture.

61

Stob Bàn (white peak), an angled prominent hill, ridge-linked to Sgorr an Iubhair via the stony-faced Corie nan Mìseach and Lochan Coire nam Mìseach (the kids corrie pool), can also be scaled from Tigh na Sleubhaich (the house of the gullied slope) in Lairig Mòr, or from Achriabhach in Glen Nevis. Approaches and summit provide a 360 degree explosion of ridge upon ridge and mountain tops that can have few equals. This includes the distant spectacles of Bidean nam Bian beyond Aonach Eagach, the reflective waters of Loch Linnhe shimmering between Beinn a' B'heithir and the heights of Ardgour, and the great mass of The Ben. There are immediate views – from the bealach of Stob Bàn's sculptured north-east buttresses and glinting scree chutes (reminiscent of the Pyrenean Grande Vignemale's north face) – above the falls, tumbles and slides of Allt Coire a'Mhusgain (burn of the corrie of the rotting wood pass). Fields and shutes of quartzite, exposed during the Ice Age when abrasive glaciers and ice flows decapitated the pinnacle rock caps, are particularly apparent on the south-western summit mounds of Stob Bàn and Sgùrr a Mhàim, and in certain lights are often mistaken for a covering of snow.

From Stob Bàn west the sweeping rims of Coire Dearg (red corrie) and Coire an Lochan (corrie of the small loch) provide an invigorating hike to Mullach nan Coirean (summit of the corries). This most westerly Mamore, in tandem with its ancillary top Meall a' Chaorainn (hill of the rowans), provides not only descents into Glen Nevis via the West Highland Way, but also unique facets of the furrowed Carn Dearg and Coire Eoghainn (Ewan's corrie) on The Ben's south face.

Distant vistas south-west over Loch Linnhe, from Stob Bàn

Opposite: Glinting quartzite chutes and the north-east buttresses of shapely Stob Bàn

4 NETHER LOCHABER, FORT WILLIAM AND BRAE LOCHABER

festina lente – hasten gently

ALTHOUGH A TOPOGRAPHICAL CONTRAST to other chapters, there remains within this boundary of loch, glen and Lochaber's capital a common bond of birth, blood and man's endeavour. Extending north and east for 32 miles (51km), from the confluence of Lochs Linnhe and Leven, it embraces the southern extremities of the Great Glen fault including Loch Linnhe and Fort William, ascending gradually from Corpach via the Caledonian Canal to Gairlochy 115ft (35m), then east with the scoured phenomenon of Glen Spean to 788ft (240m).

LOCH LINNHE AND NETHER LOCHABER

WITH THE CHURCH of St Brides behind, leave North Ballachulish via the seasonally busy A82(T), west for Onich (Gaelic, *Omhanaich* meaning place full of rich frothy milk), a ribbon of acers and azaleas, hotels and guest houses, and lochside site of the 7ft (2m)-tall Neolithic Clach a' Charra perforated standing stone. Onich combines the bustle of tourist traffic with the stunning lochside scenery into Glen Coe and the layered frieze and serrated skyline of Ardgour (Gaelic, *Aird Dhobhar* meaning the promontory of the water).

Beyond Onich, pass through tiny Glen Righ (king's glen), at the northern extremities of which lie forest trails to woodland waterfalls and Wade's Old Military Road, prior to the 'wiggle' announcing the Nether Lochaber Hotel and Highland Council's Corran Ferry. The first car ferry was built to carry two cars, by an

Loch Linnhe from Corran to distant Ben Nevis

Corran Narrows and lighthouse from Nether Lochaber jetty

ancestor of the present proprietors of the Nether Lochaber Hotel. Foot passengers and bicycles have a highly recommended free crossing, not only for the pervasive views into Glen Coe and Nether Lochaber but also for the pleasures of Ardgour. For now the hills relax and rocks have lost their jagged edges, giving way to sapphire lochs on whose birch-clad banks all manner of plant life flourishes – primrose and celandine in spring, rhododendrons and bluebell carpets from May, to autumn's varied heathers and ling.

Loch Linnhe's origins lie in the lateral displacement of the Great Glen that sliced Scotland practically in two. It's an elegant sea-loch that combines with the Firth of Lorn and Loch Eil to create the largest indentation in Scotland's west coast. The outer loch, An Linne Shieleach (the brackish channel), drops to a depth of 660ft (201m) while the upper loch, An Linne

Dhubh (the dark channel), reaches depths of 420ft (128m) and was known, centuries past, as Lochaber. Narrows – pincers of land separating the upper loch from the wider, sea-fed mouth – were formed from glacial outwash gravels. The distinctive Corran gravel fan, its lighthouse pristine white, stands 80ft (24m) above sea-level with the narrows shallowing to 36ft (11m).

It was through these narrows, centuries ago, that a MacLean of Mingary, Ardnamurchan sailed to plunder the lands of Lochaber. To ensure his boat was not recognised as he returned, this master of disguise painted the hull from stem to stern, black on one side and white on the other. Corran's flood-tides were regarded with trepidation by generations of Lochaberian landlubbers, graphically expressed by an emigrant who, in 1802, boarded a sailing ship from Fort William bound for Canada. 'Once past the narrows I will be fine' – implying the Corran surges held greater dangers than the Atlantic Ocean.

From Corran, the tree-lined A82(T), with lochside picnic area and lay-bys, soon reaches the outskirts of Fort William, marked by several miles of tourist accommodation through Achintore (Gaelic, *Ach an Todhair* meaning the field of the bleaching [of flax]). Another route into Fort William, through Upper Achintore, is via Caulfeild's Old Military Road, winding with the panoramic moorland Lundavra drove road at Blarmachfoldach, a clachan that until recent times observed the Julian calendar of 365¼ days, in which 1 January coincides with 12 January of today's Gregorian calendar.

Top: *Loch Linnhe sunset, south to Corran*
Above: *Fort William below Cow Hill, over Loch Linnhe from Corpach Basin*

FORT WILLIAM

FORT WILLIAM (*An Gearasdan* – The Garrison), Lochaber's capital and West Highland tourist and shopping centre, is a relatively modern town of 10,900 souls (if Inverlochy, Claggan and Caol are included) nestling at Loch Linnhe-head; a population that varies enormously as the seasonal visitors come and go. A functional, friendly township, it has many amenities for the visitor, including a full range of overnight facilities and specialist shops. To the north it marches with Inverlochy, and all shelter beneath the umbrose western flanks of the Nevis massif, which, despite its bulk and proximity, remains hidden by Cow Hill, Fort William's eastern sentinel and grandstand. Located at the south-western entrance to the Great Glen, with direct access to the sea, one would imagine the Fort's development stemmed from trade and travel. Although such factors influenced its growth, its difficult birth and turbulent childhood resulted from a seventeenth-century military and political marriage of convenience.

The original fort, a primitive construction, was erected in 1654 by Cromwell's man, General George Monck, as a deterrent to Clan Cameron. Monck named it Inverlochtie after the nearby ruined castle to the north; it was however spoken of locally as *An Gearasdan Dubh Inbhir-Lòchaidh* (The Black Garrison of Inverlochy).

'Fort William' came with General Hugh Mackay in 1690 when he constructed a stronger stone structure on the site of Monck's fort, armed with fifteen naval cannon and capable of housing one thousand redcoats. On completion MacKay scaled the ramparts, unfurled the royal standard and completed the affront to Lochaber by naming the redoubt Fort William after his master King William II. The illustrated 1694 William and Mary halfpenny, worth twelve times the Scots equivalent, ie the 'Bawbee' or Scots sixpence, would have been in the pay-packets of Fort William's redcoats.

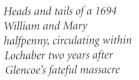

Heads and tails of a 1694 William and Mary halfpenny, circulating within Lochaber two years after Glencoe's fateful massacre

The fort was strengthened in the 1720s by General Wade, and in 1746 resisted a Jacobite siege for five weeks, suffering six killed and twenty-four wounded. In 1864 it was partially dismantled, its stones used for hospital and house building, and in 1889 it was bought by the West Highland Railway. Little remains today, save the main gateway stones, stone sea defences and pine panelling from the room in which Colonel Hill rejected Glencoe's declaration of allegiance and later authorised the Massacre.

The first settlement adjoining the 1654 fort was known as Braintoun after Colonel Brayne, later changed to Maryburgh, after William's wife Mary daughter of James VII, when the 1690 fort was reconstructed. A post office was established in 1764 and a jail in 1781. Reverend Fraser recorded in 1791, 'In Fort William there are two inns, and in almost every other houfe in Maryburgh, whysky is sold'. The Duke of Gordon acquired Maryburgh in the early 1800s, renaming it Gordonsburgh, later changed to Duncansburgh when gained by Sir Duncan Cameron – a name that reverted in 1874 to the original, greatly despised and rarely used, Fort William, Highlanders preferring the abridged 'The Fort'.

Pine panelling in this West Highland Museum room is the original from Colonel Hill's Fort William office, from which he authorised the Massacre of Glencoe. Note also the birching table, last used in 1948. The birch is a replica, the original being too worn to display

Fort William's development, kick-started albeit for the wrong reasons by Wade's and Caulfeild's military roads, was to continue apace throughout the ensuing centuries. Boundaries expanded and the industrial age arrived with the advent of Thomas Telford's Caledonian Canal 1803–22, the West Highland Railway in 1894, followed by the 1930s hydroelectric schemes, aluminium smelter and offshoot timber industries.

Enthusiasm for this industrial revolution generated a period of civil engineering and railway mania, when everything was considered and anything was possible. A rack-railway to The Ben's summit, or Fort William as an Atlantic terminus to rival Southampton and Liverpool were considered, but came to naught.

The West Highland Railway however was up and running, having arrived in Fort William from Glasgow on Saturday 11 August 1894 with much celebration. The twentieth century saw increased goods traffic and the Sunday excursion boom to Fort William from industrial Clydeside. However, the depression of the 1930s and the Second World War marked the beginning of the end, with excursions finally hitting the buffers in 1957. Happily the West Highland line continues over its 150 bridges from Corrour to the Fort, and seasonal steam has returned with the Jacobite Train chugging to Mallaig and back.

Entering Fort William from the south, its road and street signs in Gaelic and English, motorists pass a large car park alongside the loch on a bypass road, with views of the steamer pier. Branching off is a side-road to the bus and railway stations, a supermarket, further education college, a leisure centre and the ubiquitous fast-food cafeteria. All are linked to the High Street by a tunnelled walkway below the bypass road, the walkway much favoured – as is the covered footpath of the High Street (clearly for shelter rather than acoustic quality) – by saxophonists, penny-whistlers, button-box and fiddling buskers and, unfortunately, beggars.

Beyond is An Aird Stadium, venue of many a rousing shinty match, for, in the words of Sandy Slater, chairman of Fort William Shinty Club 1994, in the foreword to Hugh Dan MacLennan's *The First 100 Years*, 'Shinty has always, and will always, play a hugely influential role in the development of Fort William'. The character of the game and the club are best expressed by Hugh Dan's *Historical Highlights: Roll of Honour* of the club with such happenings as:

1645 Battle at Inverlochy.
1692 Massacre of Glencoe.
1863 Original Belford Hospital opened.
1893 Fort William Shinty Club formed.
1992 Camanachd Cup Final: Fort William 1 Kingussie 0.

The A82(T) continues, past Belford Hospital *en route* to Nevis Bridge. Up until the early 1900s the A82 squeezed through the High Street and alongside the grass, gardens and striking monuments of the Parade. Today's pedestrianised granite cobbled walkway, marked at either end with symbolic sculptures, allows safe access to the many shops and amenities. At its southern end, by Gordon Square, an incongruous sandstone sculpture, designed to depict the Fort's heritage, displays a peculiar hieroglyphic – resembling a 'C' superimposed above an 'H' – in one of the many words on its angled faces. Its presence brings to mind Dr Johnson's response in 1773 to the pretentious castle at Inveraray, in which he intimated there is little to admire save 'the total defiance of expense'. More pleasing, at the north

Top: The Parade, gardens and impressive monuments, memorial to the fallen of two world wars, and the statue of Donald Cameron of Lochiel, XXIV Chief of Clan Cameron

Above: Christmas lights decorate the pedestrianised High Street

end close by Fort William's library, is an inlaid Celtic mosaic, and in the middle, within adjoining Cameron Square, is the West Highland Museum and the Tourist Office of The Highlands of Scotland.

The four-seasons West Highland Museum opened in 1922; it was extended in 1962, and was completely revamped in 1997 when the town unashamedly celebrated in the High Street with the longest 'Strip the Willow' in the west. Small and unpretentious, it remains a giant amongst Scotland's museums, a treasure-trove of Jacobite memorabilia, rich in the life and times of Lochaber and Fort William.

A short distance north from Belford Hospital stands The Craig's burial ground on the left, preceded by a well-tended garden and an inscribed archway rebuilt from The Fort's gateway. Note the rocky outcrop behind which Jacobite cannons ineffectively bombarded The Fort in 1746.

Departure from Fort William, host to the annual Lochaber Gathering (Highland Games) and oft-held Gaelic National Festival of Music and Literature, the Mod, is via the A82(T) north over Nevis Bridge at the Glen Nevis roundabout.

Stone sculpture, alongside Gordon Square; (right) a slip of the chisel!

TO VICTORIA BRIDGE

FROM NEVIS BRIDGE NORTH-EAST we have Claggan, north of River Nevis, beyond which lies the start/finish of the gruelling Ben Race, and on the left the redundant 1898 Glenlochy Distillery of the Glenlochy-Fort William Distillery Co Ltd, all red brick and distinct towers. Inverlochy village, immediately north, was constructed in the late 1920s to accommodate workers for the new hydroelectric aluminium complex.

Redundant Glen Lochy Distillery, fine brick and elegant towers

As buildings fade look left for the green mound of Tom na Faire (look-out hill) for Inverlochy Castle, the site of Lochaber's last 'pit and gallows' – prison and hanging – execution. Opposite Tom na Faire to the east stands the 1929 aluminium smelter and power house of Alcan Smelting and Power UK, although extensive, careful siting and time have obscured the works, leaving only the downtake pipeline visible. Conducted tours through the plant can be arranged.

A feature of this industrial giant is the extent of its holdings, acquired initially for the hydroelectric schemes. Alcan Highland Estates Ltd administer Killiechonate and Mamore estates, covering the Killiechonate Forest and Mamore Forest, including Fort William and Spean Bridge golf courses, and the Nevis Range ski complex at Aonach Mòr. The estates endeavour to sustain employment whilst ensuring access to hill-walking and climbing areas.

North of Alcan's entrance a lane, signposted Inverlochy Castle, leaves the A82(T) and crosses Alcan's tailrace to old Inverlochy Castle. Beyond, the wide waters of River Lochy, enclosing a nest of colourful islets, lead the eye over the sand-flats to Caol (Gaelic, *an Caol* meaning the strait).

THE FIRST INVERLOCHY CASTLE

FROM AN EIGHTH-CENTURY TREATY between Achaius of Dalriada and Charlemagne of France, there rose through the morning mists of Inverlochy the first castle, later demolished by marauding Vikings. Today's partially restored stronghold, reputedly built in the thirteenth century by John Comyn of Badenoch, is a bastion of truly formidable presence, reflecting an unsavoury past of battles, rapes and beheadings.

Old Inverlochy Castle, knocked about a bit by Montrose in 1645

Inverlochy experienced two great battles. In 1431, Donald Balloch of the Isles tackled the might of James I, led by the Earls Huntly and Mar. At least a thousand of the king's army perished, and evidence of fleeing soldiery is encountered in Glen Nevis (see Chapter 5). The second battle of 1645 is described by many, including John Buchan in *The Marquis of Montrose* (see Bibliography, page 110).

The epic march of Montrose from Killcummin (Fort Augustus) to Inverlochy through January snow, ranks high in Scottish military history. With his 1,500 troops bottled in the Great Glen between Seaforth's rag-tag thousands and Argyll's vengeful army, he chose, with text-book tactics, to battle with Argyll. Montrose literally disappeared into the snow bound Monadhliath hills *en route* via Roybridge, through the wild tangle surrounding Ben Nevis to reappear below Meall an-t-Suidhe by Inverlochy.

Next morning the battle commenced on Goirtean Odhar (dun-coloured little field), close by Alcan's smelter, against the entire Campbell army with Achenbracke at their head. Argyll himself chose to observe from his Loch Linnhe barge. Accounts of the battle allege that Argyll lost 1,500 brave men and Montrose 10. For brevity I include extracts from two official reports. Col MacDonell: 'For only two regiments of our army, advanced till they recovered Argyle's standard and the standard bearer, at which their whole army broke.' Montrose battle report: 'Our men did wonders, and immediately came to push of pike and dint of sword, after the first firing.' He later writes (with tongue in cheek?) about the slaughter, 'which I would have hindered if possible that I might save your majesty's misled subjects.'

BEN NEVIS DISTILLERY

FOUNDED AND BUILT IN 1825 by John MacDonald from Glen Spean, this legitimised still-house, well served with 'Water, Barley, Yeast and Peat Reek' and Long John's skills, produced a *Uisge Beatha* (water of life) called the 'Dew of Ben Nevis'. Queen Victoria visited in 1848 and the distillery continues to welcome visitors.

From the distillery we have a choice of routes to Spean Bridge. The most direct sweeps north-east with the A82(T) through the Great Glen, alongside the West Highland Railway and to a lesser extent with Wade's 1736 Military Road. Alternatively, a longer journey awash with interest takes the A830(T) 'Road to the Isles' to Banavie and Corpach, then with Telford's early 1800s scenic B8004, or the Caledonian Canal, to Gairlochy.

THE SECOND INVERLOCHY CASTLE

CLOSE BY TORLUNDY, 1½ miles north from the distillery, stands the second Inverlochy Castle (locally called Torlundy Castle), an 1860s turreted Gothic mansion built by the 3rd Baron Abinger. The Inverlochy Castle estate was later sold to J. W. Hobbs who transformed it into an American-style 'Great Glen Cattle Ranch'. In 1969, the castle became a luxury country-house hotel, reputed to be Britain's most expensive.

Without doubt, on foot is the way to approach Spean Bridge, as although the train is pleasant, views are restricted. By Torlundy leave the A82(T) east, crossing the railway onto Wade's road for a spanking 6-mile (9.6km) hike, passing the slip road leading to the site of the Stirk auction mart and agricultural centre and possibly Lochaber Film Studios, prior to Nevis Range Gondola station (fulcrum for a selection of lower-level walks and cycle routes), north-east to Spean Bridge, with an option of an intriguing Jacobite experience at High Bridge. Although initially abhorred by the Highlander, Wade's highways later gained 'literary' appreciation:

> *If you had seen these roads before they were made,*
> *You would hold up your hands and bless General Wade.*

Immediately beyond Aonachan rail bridge lie alternatives, either the tree-lined lane to Highbridge, or you can walk the A82(T) to Spean Bridge – in the tourist season the most miserable mile in Lochaber.

DROCHAID ARD (HIGH BRIDGE)

HIGH BRIDGE, spanning the steep-sided Spean gorge, was under General Wade's supervision to be 'of three Arches; the Middle Arch fifty foot Diameter, and fourscore Feet from the common Surface of the Water'. Laying the first stones was recorded in a military report June 1736, when 'loyal toasts were drunk and great guns were fired'.

This crucial link in Wade's Inverness road witnessed the first skirmish of the 'Forty-Five': a classic guerrilla encounter, succinctly described, on a path-side cairn above High Bridge, by the 1745 Association. 'Donell MacDonell of Tìrnadris (Keppoch's cousin) plus 11 clansmen and a piper used the now demolished High Bridge inn and surrounding trees to rout 85 men and officers, two companies, of the 1st Regiment of Foot marching from Fort Augustus to Fort William.' This rousing tale is fictionalised in D. K. Broster's *The Flight of the Heron*.

Donell MacDonell, who fought throughout the campaign, was to lose both life and house after Culloden. Imprisoned in Edinburgh and then Carlisle, he was, on the orders of the Duke of Newcastle, brutally slaughtered in October 1746.

By the early 1800s High Bridge was in terminal decline. Today crumbling pillars teeter, dilapidated and dangerous, above a gorge colourfully carpeted with wild flowers, but sadly plagued by myriad *meanbh chuileag* (midges), causing intruders 'to fall back in some confusion'.

How could the intrepid Hon Mrs Murray in 1799 condemn this land of legends so: 'From High Bridge to Fort William is the most dreary, though not the ugliest, space I have travelled in Scotland.'

TO SPEAN BRIDGE BY ROAD AND CANAL

TAKE THE A630(T), originally a Telford road, to cross the River Lochy via Victoria Bridge, past Lochaber High School with The Ben at your back to arrow over the flats of Corpach Moss and Blàr Mòr (big moss) to Banavie and Corpach. The Caledonian Canal is crossed by road and rail swing bridges immediately below Neptune's Staircase.

CORPACH

CORPACH (Gaelic *Corpaich*, meaning the place of bodies) below Loch Eil narrows, was a staging post for revered cadavers, including early Scottish and Norse royalty, on the Great Glen coffin route to the sacred burial isle of Iona. In 1822 the Caledonian Canal opened with Corpach Basin and sea-lock as its western gateway, and in 1901 Corpach gained its railway

Opposite: Crumbling remains of General Wade's High Bridge, site of the '45s' first skirmish

The bottom lock of eight in Neptune's Staircase

station. From Corpach's sea-lock with its pepper-pot lighthouse of 1913, popular with visitors and photographers, to the top lock at Gairlochy, the canal provides 8½ miles (13.5km) of scenically impressive canal-bank walking or cycling.

THE CALEDONIAN CANAL

AFTER CULLODEN and the resultant ethnic cleansing, minds were concentrated on schemes to provide work for deposed clansmen. The trustees of the forfeited estates acted first, commissioning engineer James Watt, and in 1793 John Rennie engineer/bridge designer, to survey the Great Glen regarding possible canal construction. Their estimates however were too expensive. Continuing economic deprivation and increasing emigration prompted the Treasury to engage Thomas Telford to connect the Great Glen lochs for passage of naval ships, merchantmen and fishing boats. His report of 1802 on 'this remarkable valley' concluded that a

Opposite: Corpach beyond Caol, at Loch Linnhe's head

Below: Corpach Basin, the western extremity of the Caledonian Canal

canal 20 feet deep would take seven years and cost £350,000, later increased to £474,000.

Construction at both ends, commencing in 1803, was completed in 1822 although widening and strengthening continued between 1843–47, with a final bill of £1,201,000. Out of this came £127 7s ½d, for 'Whiskey allowed to Men working in the Water'.

The first ship to come from Inverness to Fort William on 23 October 1822, marked the official opening, with the *Inverness Courier* in the journalese of the day reporting: '67 gentlemen sat down to a handsome and plentiful dinner, after which no less than 39 toasts were proposed and drunk.' The toast to Mr Telford was nineteenth on the list and the party broke up 'with genuine highland spirit'.

Today's canal is administered by British Waterways, and interesting statistics include a total length of 60 miles (96km), 38 miles (60.8km) of natural lochs, 22 miles (35.2km) of canal cuttings and 29 locks; maximum vessel size is draught 13½ft (4m), length 150ft (45.5m), beam 35ft (10.5m). Replacement of oak/cast-iron lock gates with oak/steel gates (weighing 45 tonnes per double gate) occurred in 1887–93 and in 1998–9. In 1959–68 the lock-gate manual capstans were replaced with hydraulic rams.

The appeal of this artery of our industrial heritage, a major contributor in the birth of Scottish tourism, although condemned as obsolete before it was opened, continues to enthral and entice. Few perhaps realise that the canal was foreseen by the seventeenth-century Brahan Seer, who predicted 'that ships in full sail will pass eastwards and westwards by Muirton and Tomnahurich' (once land-locked, but now alongside the canal).

BANAVIE

RECORDED IN THE FIFTEENTH century, Banavie (place of pigs) overlooks the eight locks of Neptune's Staircase through which boats are raised/lowered 72ft (22m) – locks that lowered 512 fishing boats in 1870 westward-bound for the 'silver darlings' (herring) in the Minch. The lock-keeper's house has unusual central bay windows to observe approaching vessels, and the upper room is still known as 'Telford's room'. I could watch for hours the oak gates releasing all manner of craft, like greyhounds from a trap, into this way of black water.

Tales of Neptune's Staircase abound, none more so than the story of James Rhodes and his wicked tongue. James ran his lock-keeper's house as an inn, moonlighting – as did others – to supplement his lock-keeper's wage. This perquisite he lost in the 1880s due to his abuse showered on any steamboat whose passengers did not frequent his pub. So offensive was he, it is said, that skippers would rather risk the rigours of the Pentland Firth and Cape Wrath than face Rhodes' wrath at Neptune's Staircase.

The eight locks of Neptune's Staircase with the old gates removed prior to replacement, 1998–9

GAIRLOCHY

Autumn's tranquil evening afterglow, above the top lock at Gairlochy

AT GAIRLOCHY (SHORT RIVER LOCHY) the top lock by Loch Lochy marks the end of our canal journey. Passage continues to Spean Bridge via the B8004 and A82(T), although alternative paths can be followed from the map. From Gairlochy the B road ascends via the Bridge of Mucomir (plain of the confluence) over the 'Telford-excavated' course of the River Lochy. Once built, this elegant three-arched bridge was adopted as a main drove route into Brae Lochaber.

BRAE LOCHABER

EAST FROM THE JUNCTION OF THE A82(T) and the ascending B8004, by the striking Commando Memorial and its nearby Fiery Cross knowe, lies Glen Spean (Gaelic, *Gleann Spiathan*, meaning hawthorn glen). East-

81

Opposite: River Spean, now peaceful, enjoyed from Telford's Spean Bridge

west from Laggan dam and Tulloch (Gaelic *Tulaich*, meaning a hillock) to Gairlochy it runs, and from its pastured banks and blood-soaked braes, glimpses of the remarkable Parallel Roads can be seen.

Originally thought to be ancient Celtic Fingalian tracks, the 30ft (9m) 'Roads' are in fact shorelines of large lakes produced when a glacial advance dammed Glen Spean and its tributary Glen Roy. Shorelines of fallen rock in Glen Roy gathered at 1,148ft (350m), and as the ice retreated so did the water level to 1,070ft (326m), followed by a third at 856ft (261m). The third level, when water overflowed into Glen Spean, produced Parallel Roads at 856ft (261m), shown on OS map Landranger 41. The final breaking of the waters occurred when Glen Spean's ice retreated, gouging the gorges of Spean as it poured into the Great Glen. For further information consult J. B. Sissons, *The Evolution of Scotland's Scenery* (see Bibliography, page 110).

The Commando Memorial, a memorable and moving tribute to the 1,706 Commandos who perished during the 1939–45 conflict, was restored in 1998 to its pristine glory. Sculptured by Scott Sutherland in arresting bronze and granite on a far-seeing knowe, it is at its best awash with autumnal afterglow backed by the profiles of Nevis.

Spean Bridge below Kilmonivaig church is a bustling village of character. Telford built his fine bridge in 1819, a magnet for road builders for now we have main roads to Skye, Inverness, Kingussie and Fort William, plus the lane from Insh and Corriechoille (corrie of wood), converging on the village – with dire results during the tourist season. The village boasts an exciting stretch of river gorge, a colourful railway station with restaurant, a lively hotel and a busy, helpful tourist office.

The riverside lane to Corriechoille provides a fine start for walkers and mountain bikers for it leads to the Grey Corries and Lairig Leacach, gateway to Loch Trèig-head, Rannoch Moor and Glen Nevis.

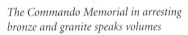

The Commando Memorial in arresting bronze and granite speaks volumes

Corriechoille is perhaps more familiar as the appellation of John Cameron the Lochaber drover, Scotland's greatest stocksman. Born around 1780, son of a toll/inn-keeper in the parish of Kilmonivaig, he rose, via the droving trade, to lease fifteen holdings from Lochiel himself, his clan chief. He died on 16 February 1856, a relatively poor man, and was buried in the family plot at Cille Choireil.

Returning to Spean Bridge, take the A86 road east for an odyssey of immense interest, via Tìrnadris (land of thorns), north of the road and below Meall nan Luath (hill of ashes), home to Donell MacDonell, Jacobite hero of High Bridge. Tìrnadris witnessed the 1610 (or 1612?) murder of five fugitive MacGregors, whose headless bodies were buried nearby.

Cille Choireil surveys Brae Lochaber

ROY BRIDGE AND MONESSIE GORGE

PASSING INVERROY we arrive at Roy Bridge, as did Argyll's Covenanters who in 1639 and 1644 cut great sectarian swathes through the 'proven enemies of religion' and in the process demolished Keppoch House and Castle. In Walter Scott's words in *Heart of Midlothian*, 'prove their doctrine orthodox by apostolic blows and knocks'.

Telford built his bridge over the River Roy in 1817 and for 149 years it stood its ground before retiring. A left turn past St Margaret's leads north to Glen Roy's three sets of Parallel Roads; Glen Spean's single level can be seen north above Tulloch and south from Monessie. East from Roy Bridge, by road or intermittent pathway, lies Monessie Gorge (Gaelic, *I m'un Easa*, meaning near the waterfall), with the West Highland line clinging to its northern rim, flanked by sylvan banking above water-worn rocks. Access by foot is from Achluachrach (field full of rushes) east beyond Glenspean Lodge, opposite St Cyril's lane and south past 'Church Key' cottage. The gorge is spectacular but requires a sure step and a level head.

CILLE CHOIREIL

AT THE ROADSIDE CLACHAN of Achluachrach, ascend the lane north-east to the bluff of Dun Aingeal (beacon fort), overlooked by Tom a' Chrochaire (hangman's hill). Here stands Cille Choireil (St Cyril's), and for those laid to rest there a Gaelic phrase is often used: *Chaidh e thar a' Mhàim* (he went over the ridge). Three cross-topped cairns flank the lane, one to Ewan MacDonell of Insh, another to Alasdair his son, and a larger inscribed cairn, 'to D. P. MacDonald, son of Long John'.

The sixth-century original, built by Choireil, nephew and disciple of Columba's, was a simple cell replaced in the fifteenth century by Ailean nan Creach. This creation of conscience, known as 'Kilkarill', was dedicated to St Choireil. Restored in the early 1930s, financed mainly by Canadian descendants of Brae Lochaber's nineteenth-century emigrants, it was re-opened by Bishop MacDonald of Victoria, British Columbia.

Within this sacred but crowded ground lie a veritable 'who's who' of Brae Lochaber, with a clutch of Celtic crosses crowning the graves of Lochaber's clergy, on Tom Aingeal (High Brae). Haunting and haunted, as church and burial ground are, there is little doubt that the whole is enhanced by an unsurpassed prospect east and south of Brae Lochaber, that as far as I am concerned, in all my wanderings throughout many lands is unequalled.

The haunting restored interior of Cille Choreil

Above: Celtic crosses adorn Tom Aingeal, Cille Choireil's upper burial ground; and (below) stone inscribed to 'Iain Lom, Bard na Ceapaich' by Cille Choireil's door

Approaching the church, for a visit within is fundamental, note the enclosed headstone, 'In Memory of John Cameron of Corrychoillie', and also by the low chapel door the upright stone inscribed with flowers, cross, harp and Gaelic verse to 'Iain Lom, *Bard na Ceapaich*' (Bard of Keppoch). The same Iain Lom guided Montrose's army through storm and snow to the walls of Inverlochy Castle. Blessed or perhaps damned with an abrasive political intellect and tongue to match, he was appointed Poet Laureate by Charles II, the only Gaelic poet with such an accolade.

Continue east, beyond Muirlaggan and Tulloch, on the unclassified road leading to Fersit and Loch Trèig, south over the River Spean to uninhabited Inverlair Lodge, in which Rudolph Hess, Hitler's deputy, was held after his ill-conceived flight from Germany in 1941. Picturesquely sited overlooking Allt Làire (mare's burn) and River Spean, a mile west of Tulloch Station and Outdoor Centre, it stands near the site of the original Inverlair House in which the seven Keppoch murderers were themselves murdered and beheaded by Iain Lom. Their bodies lie in an adjacent marked knoll; their severed heads were washed in a well alongside Loch Oich and later dispatched for display to Edinburgh. A monument marks this macabre 'Well of the Heads'.

Gory events thus conclude this chapter as the A86 rises east to Laggan Dam, and the West Highland line labours south from Tulloch ascending the slopes of Loch Trèig side; into Chapter 5 and a reunion with Chapter 1.

5 GLEN NEVIS, THE GREY CORRIES AND THE NEVIS MASSIF

ad summum – to the highest point

I T IS NOT BY CHANCE that Ben Nevis, home to the Gods of Wind and Water, and Glen Nevis, a plethora of nature's wonders, are kept until the final chapter. Afficionados and appreciative visitors know them simply as 'The Ben' and 'The Glen' – titles that simplify and classify the varying Gaelic and old Scots derivations of today's word 'Nevis'. Translations differ: Ben Nevis is Gaelic, *Beinn-neimh-bhathais* meaning hill with its head in the clouds, or again Gaelic, *Beinn-nimh-uisag* meaning the mountain of biting water; another declares descendancy from the Irish Celtic *neim*, meaning venomous one. Glen Nevis, in Gaelic, Gleann Nibheis or *Nimheis*, has Gaelic academia suggesting glen of raw and biting atmosphere/the venomous one, whereas romanticists favour the simple, glen of heaven.

Fringed by Glen Spean north, Loch Trèig (loch of destitution) east, the Mamore Forest south and Fort William and Loch Linnhe west, this

Glen Nevis south to Sgùrr a'Mhàim

A scatter of erratics beneath the southern flanks of The Ben

show-piece of Highland architecture fits comfortably into a concentrated canvas measuring 21 miles (33.5km) by 8 miles (13km). Two A-roads provide perimeter access – the A82(T) Fort William to Spean Bridge and the A86 Spean Bridge to Laggan Dam, as does the West Highland Railway via the stations at Tulloch, Roybridge, Spean Bridge and Fort William for the Grey Corries, the Aonachs, Glen Nevis and Ben Nevis. Corrour Station provides a distant gateway to the wilderness end of Loch Trèig, Lairig Leacach (slabby pass) and Upper Glen Nevis.

Two unclassified roads probe the hinterland. One is a picturesque switchback through Glen Nevis from Fort William's Nevis Bridge, of 7 delightful miles (11km) to the terminal car park below Màm Cumhann (rounded hill of the gorge) at the foot of The Ben. From the Lower Falls it is single track squeezing between Scots pine and immense boulders, where considerate sheep ease onto roadside verges to allow passage. The second, signposted Aonach Mòr, sweeps south-east from the A82(T) 7 miles (11km) north of Fort William to the Gondola station, from where skiers, mountaineers and the curious are lifted to the ski slopes.

GEOLOGY

THE BASE ROCK OF NEVIS and its supplicants, formed some 350 million years ago, are of the Devonian – Old Red Sandstone – period, when the highlands were much higher than today's Ben and covered by sedimentary schists. Internal violence then blasted surface vents through which lava poured over the layered schist, whilst colossal quantities of magma were intruded to harden far below. Subsequent cataclysms and later erosions fashioned the glens and corries, removing lava and schist to expose underlying granite prior to a final scouring 12,000 years ago, when the great Ice Cap grumbled irresistibly south-west over Lochaber, leaving in its wake visible striations and a scatter of erratics.

Today's igneous rocks form a fractured circlet of granite embracing Aonach Mòr (big ridge), the skirts of Càrn Mòr Dearg (big red hill) and Meall an t-Suidhe (hill of the sitting). Continuous refined granite envelopes the lower regions of The Ben in Glen Nevis, the stickleback of Càrn Mòr Dearg and the southern aspect of Càrn Dearg. The Ben's bonnet is comprised of some 2,000ft (610m) of andesite lavas piled high from Lochan Meall an t-Suidhe to the summit.

GLEN NEVIS

OVERLOOKED BUT NEVER OVERAWED by the fluted flanks of The Ben and the Mamores, the Glen provides a multitude of pleasing landscapes, a wealth of differing experiences and is inhabited by varied colourful wildlife. This obviously provokes assorted emotions, as anonymous quotations suggest, ranging from 'a glen on which God has turned His back', and in praise, 'Glen of Heaven'. Not quite so anonymous was the inviting Hollywood film success *Braveheart*, shot within Glen Nevis. What an invitation to 'Go see for yourself'.

The riven rock of Five Finger Gully below The Ben's summit

Access is alongside or above the twisting River Nevis (venue of the Glen Nevis River Race on the first Sunday in August), to Eas an Tuill at the lower glen's head. The initial 2 miles (3.2km) are untypical, displaying a coniferous monoculture and a roadside scatter of nesting and feeding grounds for the migratory flocks of caravans and related species. However, Forest Enterprise, with maps in Braveheart car park, provide a series of walkways/cycle tracks through Nevis Forest, including the 'Peat Track' and the concluding miles of The West Highland Way, by Dun Deardail (Deidre's fort) – a Celtic vitrified fort.

Beyond Braveheart car park and a large erratic, the Wishing Stone or Clach Shòmhairle (counsel stone), is Ionad Nibheis Centre of Natural History and Wildlife with an extensive car park. The first of five 'free' parks, unfortunately subject to the attentions of car thieves, it provides signposted access, via Achintee (field of the stormy blast), to the ascending mountain track to The Ben's summit, as does Glen Nevis Youth Hostel, with its connecting wooden footbridge and stone-stepped zigzag. Beyond the hostel the glaciated glen blossoms, stirring the senses with eye-catching exposures of the photogenic Sgùrr a' Mhàim and Stob Bàn ahead, although The Ben's summit is not visible. The riven rock of Coire Ghaimhnean (little stirk corrie), Five Finger Gully and Eas an t-Slinnein (waterfall of the shoulder), above the MacSorlie-

The overlapping Lower Falls tumble into Achriabhach gorge

Right: Glen Nevis to Sgùrr a'Mhàim from beyond the old burial ground at Ach nan Con

Cameron burial ground at Ach nan Con (field of the dogs), graces the northern skyline.

River and road swing east as white-washed Polldubh (black pit) and the tree-fringed giant steps of Leith Aire (grey point) appear left and ahead. The car park (served by a summer bus) at Achriabhach (brindled field) is the gateway to several Mamores. Nearby forked Lower Falls thunder beneath the road bridge and surge through Achriabhach gully.

Glen Nevis and its hanging valleys were originally fashioned by river water into V-shaped valleys. Later a great ice sheet growled through the glen, scouring and grinding the main valley into today's U-profiles, leaving truncated lateral valleys and over-hanging corries, particularly in the upper glen. An Steall Bhàn (pronounced 'stowl' and meaning white cascade) to be met later, one of Scotland's finest high waterfalls, pours its waters 360ft (110m) from the hanging valley of Coire a' Mhàil.

For those who seek solitude amidst a varied Highland land-scape there are few journeys that can compare with Glen Nevis, wriggling betwixt The Ben, the Aonachs, the Grey Corries, and the northern flanks of the Mamores to Loch Trèig-head. Start from Achriabhach or the terminus car park (very popular in summer) to the apparently impenetrable barrier ahead of Màm Cumhann and Sgùrr a' Mhàim; noting en route Allt Coire Eoghainn (burn of

Ewan's corrie), a 'sliding burn' of noble proportions, slipping unchecked for 1,246ft (380m) over rock inclined at 33–35 degrees from its hanging corrie. Fascinating though the slide may be, it is best for the inexperienced to observe from afar prior to following the waymarked path south-east.

Passage is possible through An Cumhang (the gorge), over whose wedged basement boulders thunders the Water of Nevis, Eas an Tuill (the falling torrent). Part walk, part scrambles this short spectacular journey is a delight in spring or autumn when silver birch, diminutive oak and Scots pine, some tall and erect, others gnarled and contorted, enhance and soften the encroaching rock. Abruptly, as these boisterous waters subside, the ravine opens onto the meadows and shingle of Steall, leading eyes and feet to An Steall's latticed white-water cascading down from Coire a' Mhàil. The river crossing to Steall Cottage (club hut and rescue post) and the foot of the falls is by courtesy of the four steel hawsers of the whimsical 'Wibbly-Wobbly-Wire Bridge'.

This unique gorge and upper glen came perilously close to extinction when, in 1960, the North of Scotland Hydro-Electric Board suggested a dam be pitched across the gorge to drown upper Glen Nevis, and the gathered water piped through the Mamores to Kinlochleven. Good sense and protest campaigns gained a temporary postponement, which became permanent in 1963.

Opposite: Glen Nevis, north from Sròn Dearg to Inverlochy, a classic glaciated valley

The author demonstrates his skill at crossing the 'Wibbly-Wobbly-Wire Bridge'

Below: Meall Cumhann in autumn garb

Allt Coire Eoghainn, a burn that slides for 1,246ft (380m) into the Water of Nevis

Opposite: An Steall's white-water hurtles from the hanging valley of Coire a' Mhàil

East beyond An Steall lies the open wilderness of upper Glen Nevis, recipient of the busy waters of Allt Coire Giubhsachan (burn of the corrie of the firs) and site of Old Steall, abandoned in the late 1930s. An ascending burn-side trod, past a hidden cauldron of cascading white-water, provides ingress to Coire Giubhsachan, a Nepalese cameo in winter, and also to distinctive Sgùrr a'Bhuic (peak of the roe-buck).

Beyond Old Steall boggy trods, with a scatter of wild orchids, await the adventurer, extending 3 miles (4.8km) to Tom an Eite (mound of the watershed) and a further 5 miles (8km) to isolated Loch Trèig-head, plus an additional 4 miles (6.4km) for the comforts of Corrour Station. I would advise anyone contemplating this trek to heed well the hours of available daylight and the proximity of the water-table.

Tom an Eite, 100yd (91m) wide, heralds what used to be known as Gleann Trèig (glen of desolation). It also has a specific Gaelic name, *Moinarmachd*, meaning moss of the armour, for here was found discarded ordnance of the Earl of Mar's defeated troops fleeing from the 1431 Battle of Inverlochy. Progress east is alongside and over Abhainn Rath (River of good fortune) in places impeded by indistinct tracks and fractious waterways

Falling torrents of the Water of Nevis thunder through An Cumhang

Right: Upper Glen Nevis looking west to the meadows of Steall

before the ruined remote Lùibeilt (steep rock corner) and adjacent Meannanach bothy are reached. At this point the way divides three ways. One ascends north, clipping the Grey Corries through adventurous Lairig Leacach and beyond to Glen Spean. The second 'four-wheel-drive' track branches south to Loch Eilde Beag and Kinlochleven, while a third continues with the true left bank of Abhainn Rath, passing Staoineag bothy and later Creaguaineach Lodge (empty) to reach Loch Trèig-head and link with Chapter 1.

THE GREY CORRIES

TRANSFIXED BETWEEN GLEN SPEAN and Glen Nevis, the Grey Corries extend south-west for some 5 miles (8km), from the breach of Lairig Leacach to Sgùrr Chòinnich Beag (Kenneth's little peak). East of the Lairig rise Cruach Innse (stack of the meadow), Sgùrr Innse (peak of the meadow), Stob a'Choire Mheadhoin (peak of the middle corrie) and Stob Coire Easain (peak of the corrie of the small waterfall), the latter towering over confined Loch Trèig. Centuries ago, Lairig Leacach funnelled south-bound cattle droves to Kingshouse over moorland now submerged by Blackwater Reservoir. Today the pass can be entered from Lùibeilt or Creaguaineach Lodge, or from Corriechoille in Glen Spean – a journey that is worth a day of anybody's time.

Seventeen tops of distinctive structured quartzite, many of them Munros, give these seldom-visited Grey Corries an appearance similar to the Mamores. The main ridge, agreeably

Top: Lairig Leacach, a winter wilderness leading to the Grey Corries

Above: Winter's grip on Clach Cartaidh, Lairig Leacach

Opposite: The Grey Corries from Leanachan Forest

benign in summer, allows a stimulating traverse west from Lairig Leacach; unfortunately such adventures are transformed into marathons due to an excessive walk in/walk out from either Glen Nevis or Glen Spean. Access to the main ridge, from the Lairig, is via Stob Coire na Ceannain (peak of the corrie of the little headland) and/or Stob Choire Claurigh (hill of the brawling corrie). Alternatively, a western approach from Glen Nevis, through Eas an Tuill to beyond Old Steall, bears north with Allt Coire a'Bhuic to the bealach west of Sgùrr Chòinnich Beag. Hill walkers contemplating the Grey Corries during the stalking season should contact the Killiechonate stalker, regarding their proposed route.

Winter in the Grey Corries upgrades hill walking into serious mountaineering, and when snow lies underfoot on Sgùrr Chòinnich Mòr (Kenneth's big peak), mind well Peter Hodgkiss in *The Central Highlands* (see Bibliography, page 110) and negotiate the eastern upper flank to avoid vicious clefts lying in wait at the ridge's northern extremity.

No account of the Grey Corries would be complete without mention of the 15-mile (24km) tunnel gouged from Loch Trèig through the Grey Corrie's skirts and the northern flanks of the Nevis range to Meall an t-Suidhe, 820ft (250m) above Fort William.

Pot still and copper worm, left anonymously on the steps of the West Highland Museum in 1924, used for illicit distilling of Uisge Beatha

Adit No 6, below Bridge 27, one of several service tunnels linked to the main water tunnel and close to the 'Puggy Line'

LOCHABER WATER POWER SCHEME

FED FROM A CATCHMENT BASIN of 303sq miles (785sq km), gathering precipitation from Laggan's 41in (104cm) per year to The Ben's 160in (406cm) per year, the Lochaber water power scheme evolved in three stages from 1921 to 1943. The first stage bored out the Loch Trèig to Fort William tunnel and re-channelled eleven burns (providing 17 per cent of the water required) running over the tunnel. The second stage dammed Lochs Trèig and Laggan and constructed a connecting tunnel, while the third stage gathered the waters of Spey into Loch Laggan.

The enormity of this civil engineering feat is illustrated by some hard facts. Loch Trèig dam raised water levels by 30ft (9m), with the tunnel from north-west Loch Trèig through the northern escarpment of the Grey Corries and Nevis range being some 79,000ft (24,079m) long with a 72ft (22m) fall and 15ft (4.5m) in diameter. Concrete-lined to reduce friction, it has valve shafts, adits and portals, prior to emerging via a surge chamber into five 6ft (2m)-diameter surface pipes descending to Fort William's power station, with 860 million gallons (3,910 million litres) flowing through daily. The power house at Fort William produces the greatest hydroelectric net output in the UK.

Construction involved drilling and boring twenty-three working granite faces. Drills were powered by air compressors, and rock was blasted by explosives – gelignite mostly. Power, transmitted by cable to the tunnel, was generated by a temporary hydroelectric station in Monessie Gorge. From 1924 some 2,000 men worked in tunnel construction and back-up services, in constructing and operating the narrow-gauge railway, in the provision of power and accommodation, and unofficially in the illicit distilling of *Uisge Beatha*.

Adits are horizontal tunnels to service tunnel boring. Shafts/intakes above the tunnel acted firstly as surge and air escape shafts, and secondly as intakes for burn water into the tunnel. Examples, together with derelict bridges, can be seen along the dismantled tramway above Corriechoille Lodge and Killiechonate, alongside the birch, rowan and myrtle-lined Allt Choimhlidh (burn of the corrie of wood), where curved trestle Bridge 27 and the bolted entrance of Adit No. 6 overlook a colourful burn. 'Choimhlidh' is not a Gaelic word, although shown as such on the OS Outdoor Leisure Map 38: it is apparently the phonetic spelling of Corriechoille.

A nearby vehicular track leads south from Bridge 27 to a conduit, intake shaft and dam over the burn, and for those who seek mountain flowers, such as purple saxifrage, the horseshoe spurs of Beinn na Socaich (hill of the pert females) and Sròn an Lochan (nose of the small loch) lie ahead. Solitude and sitings are offered of Eas Bàn (white-water) of Allt Coire a'Mhadaidh plummeting below the glinting Grey Corries, from Stob Coire Easain to Stob a'Choire Leith (peak of the grey corrie).

South-west from Allt Choimhlidh, beyond Bridge 27, the tramway continues to Allt Coire an Eòin (the bird corrie burn). From here a forest/burnside track winds south to the pipeline and a dam – the gateway into Coire an Aoin (corrie of the one) and the total isolation of An Coire Calma (brave corrie) below Aonach Beag's North-East Ridge.

THE LOCHABER NARROW GAUGE RAILWAY

BORN IN 1925 and delivered by Balfour, Beatty & Co Ltd, the 'Puggy Line' was one of Britain's longest most isolated narrow-gauge railways trundling 20 miles (32km) over the Nevis massif and Grey Corries, 656ft (200m) to 984ft (300m) above sea-level. Often close to Glen Spean's Parallel Roads, it serviced the tunnel excavations from Fort William to Loch Trèig, blowing its final whistle in 1977. What remains today is in a sad, dangerous condition and bridges in particular should *not* be traversed.

Primitive tented camps were erected close to the adits, although the camps of 'Trèig', 'Central' and 'Base' did have wooden huts. 'Central' for example, adjacent to Bridge 16, surrounded 'LC – level crossing' on today's Landranger Map Sheet 41 south from Corriechoille, and enjoyed the 'luxury' of a medical hut, kitchens, drying sheds and stores.

A 1974 report suggesting the railway as an alternative access to Aonach Mòr's ski slopes and also as a summer tourist route came to naught.

Bridge 16 of the Lochaber narrow gauge railway, adjacent to 'Central Camp', can be seen above Corriechoille

THE AONACHS

Snowgoose ski lodge, restaurant and gondola terminal – all-seasons access to Aonach Mòr

Distant Aonach Mòr above Coire Giubhsachan, from Bealach Cumhann

LINKED TO THE SOUTH with the Grey Corries, Sgùrr Chòinnich Beag, the long, high south–north ridge of the Aonachs, can be accessed from Old Steall in Glen Nevis via Sgùrr a'Bhuic and the dual peaks of Stob Coire Bhealaich (peak of the col corrie). The summit ridge is also linked by high bealach, above secluded Coire Giubhsachan, with the Càrn Dearg ridge and the omnipresent Ben Nevis. The twin summits, Aonach Beag (small ridge) and Aonach Mòr, although overlooked by The Ben, are in no way dwarfed as both top 4,000ft (1,220m). The northerly tops of Aonach an Nid (hill of the eyrie) and Sgùrr Fionnasg-aig (hill of the white-water) overlook Aonach Mòr's ski slopes and Snowgoose restaurant, with Sgùrr Fionnasg-aig the source of the oft in-spate River Cour (edge or boundary). Lachlan MacKinnon recounts a Gael's tale in his *Place Names of Lochaber*: 'When white-water has one calf a man may cross the Cour; – but when the white-water has three calves neither Fionn nor his clan can cross the Cour.'

'Aonach' is Celtic for high ground, though Aonach Mòr (the greater) at 4,006ft (1,221m) is in fact 61ft (19m) lower than Aonach Beag (the smaller)

A rather shy Aonach Beag peeps above Sgùrr a' Bhuic

at 4,067ft (1,234m). The words Mòr/Beag referred to bulk not height, which was correct as Aonach Mòr has the greater mass, although local gossip suggests topographers simply got them mixed up. This granite hill is a great snow-holder in its northern corrie of Leàc an t-Sneàchdà (slab of snow), known locally as 'Coire nan Geadh' (corrie of the goose) for, as summer approaches, its snowy rim resembles a goose's profile. It lies at the heart of Aonach Mòr's Nevis range 1990 skiing complex, serviced by a 1½-mile (2.4km) four-seasons gondola lift ascending over Leanachan Forest to Snowgoose restaurant at 2,150ft (650m). In winter it caters for 3,500 skiers with chair-lifts and tows, and provides short walks revealing the Nevis massif, Loch Linnhe, Loch Eil and beyond to Ardgour and Moidart.

The summit ridge, although wide, is steep-sided along its 1¼-mile (2km) length, particularly Aonach Beag's east face An Aghaidh Garbh (the rough face), which requires extreme care when snow-covered. Nearby North-East Ridge was conquered by W. W. Naismith and two companions for the first recorded winter ascent in 1895. The northerly Nid witnessed the slab-avalanche tragedy of 29 December 1998, in which four experienced lives were lost.

The Ben's dramatic north face seen from Torlundy, showing snow-clad cornices topping The Castle and Coire na Ciste to great effect

BEN NEVIS AND CÀRN MÒR DEARG

WHO CAN FAIL TO NOTICE the great mass of Ben Nevis above Fort William and Loch Linnhe, Britain's greatest and esteemed mountain feature? Said to have a base girth of some 24 miles (38.4km), this big-bottomed Ben, when viewed from the south, offers a rather dour aspect. Its northern quadrant however presents the reverse, with two dramatic miles (3.2km) of ridged bastions, buttresses, corries, chimneys and turrets of naked rock, up to 2,000ft (610m) in height. A Mecca for international climbers, this High Altar of British rock, snow and ice climbing (with many good guides available) sadly demands its dues, the north face apparently claiming more lives than the Eiger.

Confirmation of its exalted standing came late in life for this sleeping dinosaur, for it was not until 1847 that The Ben was declared Britain's highest. Yet to this day its actual height remains an enigma, imperially static at 4,406ft whilst continuing to exhibit metric mobility at 1,344m. Always the one to climb, Hanovarian troops in the 1700s attempted to scale it, but failed. Keats in 1818 felt 'like a fly crawling up a wainscot' and daily from June to November in 1881–82 meteorologist Clement Wragge (nickname 'Inclement' Wragge) ascended The Ben from Lochy Bridge to record weather data. By 1883 a pony track to the summit had been laid for the observatory and adjacent temperance hotel. As Nevis mania increased, W. W. Naismith's (of the time and distance formula) 1892 tussle with Tower Ridge was recognised as The Ben's first mountaineering achievement, and a year later a 'rack' railway, 4³/₄ miles (7.5km) long with a maximum gradient of 1 in 2.62, was proposed but never materialised.

Rock-hounds, hill walkers, a Ford Tourer car, a horse-drawn cart and a wheelbarrow all succeeded, followed around 1980 by pianos and barrels of beer, carried (at different times) up, but not down, by local strongman Kenneth Campbell of Ardgay.

Of all who climb The Ben, by whatever route and whatever means, one group, the Ben Runners and one individual, Bert Bissell MBE, holder of the World Methodist Peace Award, deserve special mention.

Bert Bissell of Dudley and Lochaber, erected the peace cairn of remembrance on the summit of Ben Nevis on VJ-Day at the end of the Second World War and from that date climbed The Ben twice yearly, totalling 107 pilgrimages, to lay poppy wreaths for world peace at the summit cairn. He died on the 2 November 1998, aged ninety-six.

The Ben Nevis Race 1998 – runners ascending above the Red Burn with a background of Meall an t-Suidhe and its lochan

BEN NEVIS RACE

STARTING POINTS OF THIS RACE have changed over the years but not the day – the first Saturday in September. 1895's inaugural race was to the summit only, and in its early years octogenarian D. Forbes of Fort William celebrated his ascent within three hours by dancing the Highland Fling on the summit observatory roof. The observatory closed in 1904 and so did the race, although previously it had developed into an up-and-down race from Fort William post office. The 1903 record of 2hr 10mins 19secs by Ewan Mackenzie of Achintore stood for many years. Resurrected in 1937, missing four years due to the Second World War, the race flourished and in 1981 included women.

They come to Fort William to run up the Ben
These wild mountain women and mad mountain men
    The Last Mount Richard M. Gaunt

In 1998 365 heroes took part, with local runner John Brooks of Lochaber Athletic Club the winner with a fine time of 1hr 27mins 24secs, coming very close to the 1984 record of 1hr 25mins 34secs by Ken Stuart of Keswick. The same year also established the women's record of 1hr 43mins 25secs by Pauline Howarth, Keswick Women. Two members of the Lochaber club also had reason to celebrate in 1998: Donald Paterson lowered a knee whilst descending to ask an ascending Chloe Valentine to be his bride. It was an offer, once repeated, she couldn't refuse and with heart pounding and spirits high Donald hurtled down to finish an engaged 21st and fiancée Chloe a surprised and smiling 262nd. Who said The Ben is not romantic!

WEATHER ON THE BEN

WEATHER IS A FICKLE BESOM, as the records of Ben Nevis Observatory 1883–1904 show. Direct sunshine is a shy bird on the summit with only 756 hours per year. Temperatures are on the low side, averaging fractionally below freezing over a twelve-month period, with February and March shivering well below zero, whilst July, the warmest month, basks in 42°F

Castle Ridge on The Ben's north face above a tormented Allt a'Mhuilinn

(4.5°C). Temperatures at height are influenced by the wind chill factor, and the lapse rate – every 1,000ft (305m) of ascent reduces the temperature by 3°C. Wind on The Ben is a major player, with gales gusting from 80–150mph (128–240kmph) recorded, causing mountaineers to compare The Ben with the Himalayas.

Precipitation comes to mind when considering an ascent – yearly averages register in the region of 158in (400cm), although 1898 splashed in with a staggering 240in (610cm). December leads with 19–20in (48–51cm) whilst April to June continue to be the driest months. Winter snows blanket the peak to depths of between 54in (137cm) and 140in (355cm), most clearing from the summit by July although gullies and crevasses hold snow throughout the year. All of which indicates that May and June provide the best conditions, although I have enjoyed perfect days in March, August and November.

Wm T. Kilgour, in his very readable *Twenty Years on Ben Nevis*, circa 1905 (see Bibliography, page 110), records not only unique meteorological data, but also his own idiosyncratic opinions on those who venture forth. On dehydration: 'Thirst is the constant companion of the quasi-mountaineer but the craving must be fought against at all hazards, and it will usually be found that a little of the lemon juice will act as a panacea.' On meteorologist's recreation: 'By joint action stones weighing nearly half a ton would be forced over, and what a din and commotion ensued.' Oh dear!

TODAY'S ROUTES

BEN NEVIS ATTRACTS MANY: they come in their thousands – ramblers, sponsored walkers and pilgrims – to say they have been 'up The Ben' via what they think of as the Tourist Track. Many are unaware of what the 14-mile (22.5km) traditional ascent of 4,406ft (1,344m), that can take the inexperienced hill walker up to 5 hours and the descent 2½ hours, holds in store. Heaven knows what the indigenous fox, wild cat, mountain hare, stoat, weasel, rat, mouse, soaring raptor, ptarmigan, raven and 'hoodie' crow think, not to mention the odd butterfly, bluebottle and midge. It is for this very reason that an incentive is afoot, instigated and led by the Lochaber Mountain Rescue Team, to rename the track the 'Mountain Track', in order to encourage those who ascend The Ben to understand it is not a Sunday stroll but a mountain experience, to be treated accordingly – and in doing so provide an enjoyable and no doubt unforgettable experience.

The Mountain Track ascends from Achintee and/or the Youth Hostel, stone-stepped towards Lochan Meall an t-Suidhe, then south to cross Allt na h-Urchaire (Red Burn). Beyond, zigzags in the vicinity of Coire Ghaimhnean and above the cleavage of Five Finger Gully require caution in winter and when visibility is poor. Alternatively there are longer, more challenging routes that involve some rock scrambling and a traverse of, what is for me, one of Scotland's finest narrow ridges. All pass alongside or over Allt a'Mhuilinn (mill burn – local name, whisky burn) and the solid CIC (Charles Inglis Clark) hut at 2,200ft (670m), beneath the awesome rock of The Ben's north face, reached from Lochan Meall an t-Suidhe, The Ben Nevis Distillery or the signposted North Face Car Park 750m south from Torlundy, initially along the rail bed of the 'Puggy Line'. One climbs sharply from Coire Leis (leeward corrie) to the Abseil Post, the other leads via Càrn Mòr Dearg onto the pink granite of the Arête (sharp ridge) leading to the Abseil Post topping Coire Leis. The Arête, ringed by the finest mountain scenery imaginable, requires careful placement of the feet in summer: in winter it is a journey for the ice-climber. From the Abseil Post, The Ben is ascended over steep, boulder-strewn slopes.

Càrn Mòr Dearg, a 4,000-footer (1,219m), and Càrn Dearg Meadhonach (middle red hill), highlight the long north–south ridge spilling west to Allt a'Mhuilinn and steeply east into the tight defile of Allt Dàim (reservoir burn); it is also reached from Glen Nevis, via Allt Coire Giubhsachan into Coire Giubhsachan (little fir corrie).

Hopefully your ascent of Britain's Olympus will be on a far-seeing day, when not only the entire contents of this guide in all their Highland glory will be revealed, but also a tempting panorama of Scotland's Highlands, including in a circle from the east Ben MacDui, distinctive Schiehallion, Ben More, Ben Lomond, Ben Cruachan, Skye's jagged Cuillin, Torridon's Liathach and Beinn Eighe.

And for those who admire from afar, and I would advise with the rising or setting sun, Ben Nevis is seen to advantage from Cow Hill above Fort William, Corpach Basin on the Caledonian Canal, or Upper Banavie to Muirsheerlich on the B8004 revealing the northern buttresses and precipices. A further vantage-point of the entire massif is the charismatic Commando Memorial above Spean Bridge.

From Meall Cumhann beyond Sloc nan Uan to the seldom-seen razor edge of Càrn Mòr Dearg Arête and the hazed summit of The Ben

The Bens, the glens, the lochs, Fort William and all their scenic surrounds have a wealth of experiences to offer the eager and curious visitor; and what better way to conclude this guide than to recall the Chinese proverb, which has much to say about this corner of the Highlands: 'He who deliberates before taking a step will spend his entire life standing on one leg.'

USEFUL INFORMATION AND PLACES TO VISIT

MAPS

Ordnance Survey: Outdoor Leisure 38, 1:25 000, Ben Nevis & Glen Coe Landranger 41, 1:50 000, Ben Nevis, Fort William & surrounding area
Harveys: Superwalker, 1:25,000, Glen Coe
Superwalker, 1:25,000, Ben Nevis

LOCAL NEWSPAPERS

Lochaber News
Oban Times Press & Journal

SCOTTISH HIGHLANDS TOURIST INFORMATION CENTRES

General information, accommodation from hotels to campsites and a book-a-bed service. Fort William is also a ticket agency for Citylink/National Express, Cal-Mac ferries and a Bureau de Change.

Fort William: (open all year)
Cameron Square, Fort William PH33 6AJ
Tel: 01397 703781 Fax: 01397 705184

Spean Bridge: Spean Bridge, Inverness-shire PH34 4EP
Tel: 01397 712576 Fax: 01397 712675

Ballachulish: Albert Road, Ballachulish PA39 4JR
Tel: 01855 811296 Fax: 01855 811720

A comprehensive list of specialist outdoor/indoor activities, shops, places to eat etc is included in the annual *Local Accommodation and Visitor Guide* – Fort William & Lochaber, produced by the Tourist Board and available from Tourist Information Centres.

GETTING ABOUT

Train: Glasgow via the scenic West Highland Railway, also, at the time of writing, a regular sleeper service from London. The Jacobite steam train operates a return from Fort William to Mallaig, June–Sept.

Tickets and reservations, Booking Office, Fort William Station or Tel: 01397 703791
Rail and fares information Tel: 0345 48 49 50
Auto Shuttle Express (car carrier) Tel: 0990 502309

Coach : A regular long-distance service operates from Edinburgh and Glasgow to Fort William and beyond. Services will stop on request between listed destinations.
Timetables and Reservations:
Citylink (including Skye-Ways) Tel: 0990 50 50 50
National Express (booking) Tel: 0990 80 80 80
Nearest booking agent
Tel: 0990 01 01 04
Local bus services and post bus, information from tourist information centres and bus stations. The post bus connects with the West Highland Railway.

Ferry Services: To the Hebrides linked by train from Fort William, Caledonian MacBrayne Tel: 01475 650100

Caledonian Canal: British Waterways, Caledonian Canal, Seaport Marina, Muirtown Wharf, Inverness IV3 5LS
Tel: 01463 233140 Fax: 01463 710942

Armada Yachts: 18 Glasdrum Road, Fort William PH33 6DD
Tel: 01397 700008

West Highland Sailing: Laggan Locks, Spean Bridge, Inverness-shire
Tel: 01809 501234

Corran Ferry: Highland Council. All-year daily (except 1 January), vehicular and pedestrian service

YOUTH HOSTELS

Loch Ossian Tel: 01397 732207
Glen Coe Tel: 01855 811219
Glen Nevis Tel: 01397 702336

MOUNTAINEERING HUTS

Blackrock Cottage, White Corries (Ladies Scottish Climbing Club)
Lagangarbh, Altnafeadh (Scottish Mountaineering Club)
Waters Cottage, Kinlochleven (Fell/Rock Climbing Club)
MacIntyre Memorial Hut, Onich (BMC & MC of Scotland)
Manse Barn, Onich (Lomond Mountaineering Club)
CIC Hut, Allt a'Mhuillinn GR 167 772 (Scottish Mountaineering Club)
Steall Cottage, Glen Nevis (Lochaber Mountaineering Club)

MOUNTAIN SEARCH AND RESCUE

Tel: Freephone 999 (Police) to alert and co-ordinate rescue services
Belford General Hospital, Fort William
Tel: 01397 702481

WEATHER FORECASTS

Scottish Meteorological Services:
Glasgow Weather Centre – Tel: 0141 2483451
WeatherCall 7 Day – Tel: 0891 505351
MarineCall 5 Day – Tel: 0891 505351
Ski Reports and Avalanche Update – Tel: Glencoe, 09001 654 658
Nevis Range 09001 654 660

Television and Radio: BBC 1 Scotland: Five-day forecast, 18.55hrs Mon–Fri Hill walking, skiing and sailing 18.55hrs Fri BBC 1 and 2 Ceefax 402 ITV Scotland Channel 3: Daily forecasts, Mon–Fri Teletext 154 BBC Radio Scotland FM: Daily Forecast, hill walker's forecast Friday 19.30hrs Saturday/Sunday 07.03hrs. Radio Nevis Daily Forecast FM 96.6

Climber's forecast, Teletext 159
Scottish Avalanche Information Service: Reports posted at Glencoe: ski-centre, local inns and youth hostel Fort William and Spean Bridge: tourist board office, Nevis sport, hotels, Nevis range ski-centre, hostels and bunkhouses.

DEER STALKERS

Estates and Contacts

Blackmount Estate (Chapter 1)
Contact Hamish Menzies Tel: 01838 400225; Ian MacRae, Tel: 01838 400269

Rannoch Deer Management Association (Chapter 1)
Contact Nicholas Thexton, Gaur Cottage by Rannoch Station Tel: 01882 633248

Black Corries Estate (Chapters 1 and 2)
Contact Peter O'Connel, Black Corries Estates Tel: 01855 851272

Dunan Estate (Chapter 1)
Contact Colin Robertson, Dunan Lodge, Rannoch Station Tel: 01882 633266

Corrour Estate (Chapter 1)
Contact Ted Piggot, Head Stalker, Corrour Estate Tel: 01397 732200

Glencoe and Dalness Estate (Chapter 2)
Contact The Ranger, Achnacon House, Glencoe Tel: 01855 8117

Forest Enterprise (Chapter 2)
Millpark Road, Oban, Argyll PA34 4NH
Tel: 01631 566155

Forest Enterprise (Chapter 4)
Torlundy, Fort William PH33 6SW
Tel: 01397 702184

Killiechonate and Mamore Estate (Chapters 3, 4 and 5)
Contact Mamore Stalker Tel: 01855 831511; Killiechonate Stalker Tel: 01397 712547

MISCELLANEOUS ADDRESSES

The Mountaineering Council of Scotland
4a St Catherine's Road, Perth PH1 5SE
Tel: 01738 638227

Historic Scotland
20 Brandon Place,
Edinburgh EH3 5RA

Scottish Natural Heritage
16 Hope Terrace,
Edinburgh EH12 9DQ

Scottish Rights of Way Society,
John Cotton Business Centre,
10/2 Sunnyside,
Edinburgh EH17 5RA

Scottish Youth Hostels Association
7 Glebe Crescent, Stirling FK8 2JA
Tel: 01786 891400

PLACES TO VISIT

Aluminium Story
Kinlochleven Visitor Centre, Linnhe Road, Kinlochleven PA40 4SJ
Tel: 01855 831663 (Open Apr–Oct)

Ben Nevis Distillery
Visitor Centre, Lochy Bridge,
Fort William PH33 6TJ
Tel: 01397 700200 (Open all year)

Confectionery Factory
Visitor Centre, Old Ferry Road, North Ballachulish, Fort William PH33 6RZ
Tel: 01855 821277 (Open all year)

Glencoe and North Lorn Folk Museum
Glencoe Village (Open May–Sep, Mon–Sat)

Glencoe Ski Centre
White Corries, Glencoe, PA39 4HZ
Tel: 01855 851226 (Open all year)
Scottish Skiing and Mountaineering Museum. Chair-lift and restaurant

Highland Mystery World
Glencoe, near Fort William PA39 4HL
Tel: 01855 722295 (Open Mar–Oct)

Ionad Nibheis Centre
Glen Nevis Visitor Centre,
Fort William PH33 6PF
Tel: 01397 700774 (Open Mar–Nov)
Natural history and wildlife

Lochaber Walking Festival
Inaugurated May 1999, details from tourist offices and *Lochaber News*

National Trust for Scotland – Glencoe
Glencoe Visitor Centre, Glencoe, PA30 4HX
Tel: 01855 811307 (Open Apr–Nov, Christmas/New Year)

Nevis Range Cable Cars
Torlundy, Fort William PH33 6SW
Tel: 01397 705825 (Open mid Dec–mid Nov)

Seal Island Cruises
The Pier, Fort William PH33 7NG
Tel: 01397 705589 (Open Apr–Oct)

West Highland Museum
Cameron Square, Fort William PH33 6AJ
Tel/Fax: 01397 702169 (Open all year)

FURTHER READING

Ashton, Steve, *The Hillwalker's Handbook* (Crowood Press 1987, PB 1990)

Baxter, Colin and Crumley, Jim, *Glencoe – Monarch of Glens*, (Colin Baxter Photography Ltd, 1990)

Brown, Hamish, *Walks in the Glencoe – Fort William Area* (Jarrold/OS 1992, revised 1996)

Butterfield, Irvine, *The Famous Highland Drove Walk* (Grey Stone Books, 1996)

Crumley, Jim, *Among Mountains* (Mainstream Publishing Company Ltd, 1993)

Everet, Roger (series editor), *Rock & Ice Climbs – Ben Nevis, including Aonachs, Grey Corries, Mamores, S. M. C. Climbers Guide* (Scottish Mountaineering Trust, 1994)

MacGill, Patrick, *Children of the Dead End* (Herbert Jenkins 1914, Caliban Books, 1985)

McNeish, Cameron, *The Munro Almanac* (Lochar Publishing, 1991)

Morton, H. V., *In Search of Scotland* (Methuen & Co. Ltd 1929, 26th edition 1941)

Stevenson, Robert Louis, *Kidnapped* (W. & R. Chambers Ltd 1980, first published 1886)

Storer, Ralph, *50 Best Routes on Scottish Mountains* (David & Charles 1994; as 100 Best Routes, 1987)

Full circle to lonely Rannoch Moor